Eating Well for Next to Nothing

Eating Well for Next to Nothing

by Ceil Dyer

 MASON / CHARTER   NEW YORK 1977

Library of Congress Cataloging in Publication Data

Dyer, Ceil.
   Eating well for next to nothing.

   Includes index.
   1. Cookery.   I. Title.
TX652.D94   641.5'52   76-58833
ISBN 0-88405-490-X

Contents

Introduction

The first principal of eating well for less is to cook what's in season, plentiful and therefore cheaper, and to cook *what's on hand*. I remember very well a luncheon served to me by a friend in her lovely, old country-house kitchen. It was late summer and tomatoes were ripe and plentiful so we began with a plate of sliced homegrown tomatoes sprinkled lightly with salt, a few drops of oil and chopped parsley. While we ate the tomatoes, she placed a clove of garlic, a handful of chopped parsley and a handful of fresh basil (both grown in pots just outside the kitchen door) along with about a quarter cup of oil in the blender for an instant sauce verde for the spaghetti that was to come. When we were ready, the spaghetti was tossed into a big pot of boiling water and cooked briefly until just *al dente*. Drained and served immediately with a spoonful of the sauce and a sprinkling of freshly grated Parmesan cheese, it was an experience in eating to remember, but the cost for the four of us was less than two dollars. It was a perfect example of "Eating Well for Next to Nothing."

We Americans insist on buying tomatoes in January, cabbage in June, mushrooms and oranges in July. If it isn't available then we turn to frozen foods; vegetables in so-called butter sauce, macaroni and cheese dinners, corn and spinach soufflés, precooked and frozen meats. We then continue to add all sorts of nonessentials, such as snacks, soft drinks, jellies and jams, packaged cereal and frozen coffee cake, rolls and waffles. No wonder we scream when we have to pay the tab.

Europeans have always had to be careful with food even if price were not the object; there often wasn't that much food to be had at any price. Yet anyone who has sampled a perfect Irish stew, or a real English steak and kidney pie, or just-cooked Italian pasta has never felt deprived. Bouillabaisse, that delight of gourmets all over the civilized world, is simply the result of the thrifty French fishermen's wives cooking whatever scraps of fish were not sold from the day's catch.

Learn to shop as the Europeans do. First shop your own kitchen—what's on hand, what's leftover that might be used; then and only then do your shopping, not with a preconceived menu but first to see what's best, freshest and cheapest in the marketplace.

Eating for next to nothing is a matter of revising your thinking from years of abundant food at relatively low cost, to facing up to soaring prices, to realizing that to eat well within any type of sane budget requires thought, skill, know-how, and the willingness to acquire a knowledge of food that goes beyond the buying of steaks, chops, roasts and the like. It's a matter, too, of rejecting the super-sell of the food processors and manufacturers of such products as aluminum foil, plastic bags, dust sprays, sprays to mask odors, paper towels, etc. These are major contributors to a heavy toll at the check-out counter, and they contribute nothing at all to eating well.

If instead we approach food shopping determined to buy food, not packaging, we are much more likely to eat well for far less. A famous chef once said to me, "There is always something fresh available." For example, fall and winter brings us bargains in carrots, onions, potatoes, cabbage, leeks, cranberries, bananas and a whole range of citrus fruits. Pork is likely to be less expensive and there's usually a drop in the price of cheese. As spring and summer approach fresh peas and string beans, green onions and asparagus, new potatoes and the first of the summer berries and fruit begin to appear at seasonal prices. Rhubarb, one of the earliest of the spring fruits, is usually neglected by all but the most sophisticated cooks, yet it makes the best deep-dish pie ever concocted and it has the bonus of being wonderfully rich in vitamins and minerals. Stewed with just a little sugar it is marvelous as a breakfast fruit, but it is ignored in favor of lifeless frozen orange juice. Spring and summer bring a drop, too, in the price of turkey, as versatile as chicken and usually forgotten after Christmas. Fresh fish are also usually cheaper as warm weather approaches.

Nor is better food for less a lot of trouble or work. It takes no more effort to steam quarters of fresh green cabbage than it does to heat vegetables in butter sauce; and it is no more than a few minutes work to make a pot of fresh applesauce in favor of a jar of high–priced jam or jelly.

One could go on endlessly about the virtues of buying in season but that would be a bore. There is of course more to eating well on less than simply buying what's fresh and available, but it is a key factor in saving money at the check-out counter. However, there are other equally important aspects to the battle of the food budget and here are the guidelines that I have found helpful to me. As in any endeavor, determination is the key to success; once you make up your mind, as I did, that you are sick of astronomically high grocery bills, you will find it easy to revise your thinking about food and its preparation. And if you should become a true gourmet in the process then that's all to the good, isn't it?

- Always buy what's in season, fresh, plentiful and cheap.

- Change your thinking about having to serve meat of some kind everyday. (See menu suggestions for easy, delicious substitutes.)

- Never buy processed, packaged, frozen, precooked foods. You are paying for built-in maid service and are losing on taste and nutrition.

- Mix your own cakes, waffles, cornbread, pancakes, etc. It takes practically the same time as preparing them from a mix and the cost is cut drastically.

> • Meals don't have to consist of meat, potato, two vegeta-
> bles, a salad and dessert. It's a lot more pleasurable to
> dine as the Europeans do on two or three courses of
> really interesting food.
>
> • Learn to make stock. If this sounds like a bore and a lot
> of work, it isn't, and real honest stock is the secret of fine
> French cooking as well as the secret of imparting superb
> flavor to inexpensive food. Once you try having chicken
> and beef stock on hand, you'll never be without it; fur-
> thermore, you get top nutrition and super flavor for
> pennies, for good stock is made from what most people
> throw away.

Learn to revise your thinking about cooking and try to see
how you can cut the expense of a recipe without cutting down
on the results. For example, most recipes for sautéed chicken
call for a combination of oil and butter which is then heated in
a sauté pan; the chicken pieces are browned in the hot oil,
then transferred to a warm platter to await preparation of the
sauce in which it will be sautéed. The next step in most recipes is to pour out and *discard* the remaining oil in the pan.
What a waste! With the price of oil and butter so high, it's not
just a waste—it's a crime. Did you know that the chicken
pieces (and meat for stew and ragouts as well) can be browned
in their own fat simply by placing them in the sauté pan and
putting the whole thing in a preheated 400°F oven? The heat
releases the fat from the meat or chicken, and a single turning,
to brown evenly on both sides, is all that is necessary to nicely
brown them to perfection. The excess fat in the pan is then
discarded and you have accomplished two purposes—
browned the meat and eliminated the highly saturated animal
fat that's certainly not needed in anyone's diet.

Don't go food shopping when you are ravenously hungry;
wait until after lunch or after a good breakfast. It takes super-
human will power to keep from picking up that extra hors
d'oeuvre, that tempting-looking frozen dessert or the out-of-
season strawberries.

Be knowledgeable about spices and seasonings. Many so-
called budget recipes call for half a dozen different ones—

that's no longer necessary; the mixed Italian herbs and the Spice Parisienne now on the market do away with the need for a row of herbs and seasonings which all too often get stale before they are completely used. Incidentally, the place to keep *any* seasoning is *not* over the kitchen stove but in the refrigerator where they stay fresh far longer. Add to the mixed seasoning a good brand of curry powder (Sun Brand from India is my favorite), a really hot chili powder (for an extra fiery one order from Five Alarm Chili Powder, Austin, Texas), iodized salt and a coarsely ground black Java pepper for a virtually complete spice shelf.

Liquid seasonings can be limited to soy sauce, Worcestershire sauce and homemade hot pepper sauce. Beyond these seasonings and sauces all that's needed for most good cooking are the fresh flavorings of garlic, onions, carrots and parsley, lemon juice and grated lemon rind. It's a smart idea to grate lemon rinds as you use them; store in a plastic container and freeze. You can freeze extra chopped parsley, too, but I prefer the fresh. As for seasoning most desserts, pies, cakes, cookies, soufflés, crêpes, etc., I find that a touch of brandy and sometimes a little grated lemon peel gives far more flavor than all the spices put together and the cost is actually less.

Don't throw out anything edible; vegetable leftovers can make beautiful soufflés or they can go in the stock pot. Bits and pieces of leftover meat, turkey or chicken can be finely ground, mixed with chopped pickles and celery, moistened with just a bit of mayonnaise and made into a sandwich to accompany a hearty cold or hot soup which you have made in minutes from clear, fat-free stock, and Sunday night's supper is served—a meal from what you might have thrown away.

Buy what packaged foods you must with extra care. Natural brown rice is just as easy to cook, is far better for you, tastes twice as good, and is half the price of the so-called precooked variety. The same rule of look before you buy applies to cereals. If you are a cereal addict try to stick to the old-fashioned brands that have not been gussied up. You are paying a fortune for sugar-frosted whatnots and they taste awful. Try some of the old-fashioned hot cereals for a change like Cream of Wheat, for example; a box seems to last forever and there's nothing like a hot cereal on a frosty morning. Coffee, too, is something to watch; skip the instants unless you drink very little coffee. They are an extravagance. Try to buy coffee in the bean and grind your own. Use a glass filter pot with a filter paper; Chemex, Melita, Mr. Coffee are all good. Pulverize your coffee to a powder and use one-third less. It will be just as strong and taste much better. Because the oil has been filtered out, this coffee can be saved and reheated without tasting like old tennis shoes if it's stored in the refrigerator in the interim. If you live near an A & P market buy the 3-pound bag of their Bokar coffee in the bean, less than a dollar a pound in this size bag as I write this, and really great coffee. Store all coffee in the refrigerator—it's perishable stuff.

Never buy packaged gelatin or pudding mixes; both reek of preservatives and/or artificial flavor. A box of unflavored gelatin will make six jellied salads or desserts that really taste like something, and the same milk wasted on the pudding mix can be combined with a couple of eggs and some sugar to make a delicate and delicious baked custard all for less than half the price.

As for packaged coffee cakes, sweet rolls, waffles, etc., they belong anywhere but on the gourmet's shopping list. Foolishly extravagant, they are a shameful waste of money. A twice-a-month session making rolls and coffee cakes for the freezer takes no more than a few hours time and costs about ten percent of the commercial variety. Need I mention taste?

Finally, have you looked into a bit of foraging on your own? A classic example of how people ignore what is in front of their eyes was the man in Florida who told me he had an avocado tree in his garden that was so prolific he had to use a shovel to dispose of the fruit lying on the ground. "I've never eaten one though," he said. "I don't think I would like them." Needless to say I haven't recovered yet. A farfetched example, I'll admit, but there are thousands of people who live within walking distance of the ocean, a lake or brook who never dream of spending a weekend afternoon fishing or crabbing. The same people buy frozen fish fillets in the supermarket and expensive canned crab meat. Maybe you hate the idea; if fishing is your idea of nothing at all, then try what worked for me in Charleston, South Carolina. I asked around a bit to find some young man who liked to fish and was rewarded by a supply of fresh fish and crabs every weekend. He cleaned the fish, too, and would help me boil the crabs. The price? For two or three whole fish and a dozen crabs, less than three dollars.

Often there are farms in your area that have an overabundant supply of fruits and vegetables and will give you a terrific bargain if you will come out and pick your own. Every June we pick a few quarts of vine-ripened strawberries on Saturday mornings; watermelon, corn, and tomatoes come along in July and August, and fall brings apples, pumpkins, squash and cabbage. The price is usually one-third of the supermarket's price and the fresh-from-the-picking taste is simply indescribable. Children usually love these expeditions, so if you hate the idea for yourself load the car with neighborhood children, take along a few peanut butter sandwiches and some lemonade and let them have at it—they think it is a picnic. *You* can stay in the car reading Agatha Christie or whatever.

Lastly, don't forget what's really free: beach plums and blackberries to pick wild for the best jam in the world, dandelions to make a super salad ingredient, and citrus melons (these grow in the fields in South Carolina) to transform into chutney that surpasses even the best of the mango variety. These are only a few suggestions. Naturally, what's free depends on where you live, but it pays to do a bit of inquiring.

Also under the heading of what's free could come the food you grow yourself. Yes, I know it's not really free, but the small price of a few seedlings or seeds plus a bag of fertilizer is a tiny percentage of what the results would cost. Even a small piece of ground can support a few tomato bushes, the new compact varieties bear beautiful fruit. Herbs and green onions are simple to grow even in pots. In fact, I know one girl in

Charleston who fills her window boxes with parsley every spring; the lacy dark green of her bushy, healthy plants is very attractive and she has fresh parsley in abundance until frost.

The whole point to cutting your food costs is not simply to save money. Rather, it is to control your own money to use it for what *you* want, whether it's a new car, a fur coat or your children's education! It's yours. You've earned it so you should have the privilege of using it for what you want, not have it simply taken away from you by the high-pressure sell of what has become big business, the food business. Get your food costs back under your control and if you want to use the savings for a fillet of beef or caviar and champagne, *you* at least will make the decision, for the decision is yours to make. You can indeed eat well for next to nothing if you are determined to do so.

LARGE ECONOMIES

Do you know how much you are really spending on food?

Shop for food separately. Buy all *nonfood* items, paper towels, cleaning supplies, drugs, etc., on a separate shopping trip. You'll be amazed at how much you are spending on these *nonfoods* and you will automatically cut down.

Eliminate unnecessary *nonfoods* wherever possible; paper towels, for example, can be handy, but try cutting them out in favor of a few tea towels that can be easily thrown in the washing machine. Wrap salad greens, sandwiches, unfrosted cakes, unbaked ice box cookies, etc., in damp tea towels and store in the refrigerator. Use brown paper bags to drain fried foods. Skip aluminum foil in favor of cooking utensils with lids; buy a set of inexpensive covered glass containers to store leftovers and beef or chicken stock, or use mason jars or clean cottage cheese and sour cream containers.

Skip the frozen food counter completely. Frozen orange juice may be cheaper than fresh, but it far less valuable in minerals and other nutrients as well as inferior in taste. Buy fresh oranges or grapefruit by the bag in season and have the real thing. Substitute a bowl of other fresh fruit in the summer when fruit is cheap and plentiful and oranges are high and not at their best. Frozen food is nearly always high in price and low in taste and nutrition. Stick to fresh in-season foods. As for TV dinners, beef or chicken pies, "sauced vegetables," frozen fish, etc., they are an insult to the taste buds and the pocketbook.

Some canned goods are good buys but approach with caution. Canned tomatoes and tomato juice are usually a bargain. Buy the largest can, use what's needed and store the rest in clean mason jars in the refrigerator (use within ten days). Cream-style corn is usually another bargain and so are sliced beets. Try an onion, beet and orange slice salad for a winter change.

Cut out soft drinks, candy, chewing gum, cookies, potato chips, snacks of various kinds. This may sound awfully Spartan, but a big pitcher of ice tea with fresh lemon slices and fresh mint on hand in the refrigerator takes only seconds and pennies to make and is twice as refreshing as colas, uncolas or "the real thing." If you substitute plain saltines with a wedge of real cheese for the potato and corn chips, I believe you will enjoy it twice as much. As for candy bars and chewing gum, forget them in favor of a homemade cookie or a slice of applesauce cake—who knows, the teeth you save may be your own.

High on the list of "don't buys" are gravy, sauce or salad dressing mixes, canned soups, so called "hamburger extenders," packaged macaroni dinners, prepared salad dressing particularly the kind billed as Italian, French or blue cheese. However, some brands of commercial mayonnaise (I like Hellmans best) can be a good buy depending on the current price of salad oil; it is a certain amount of trouble to make, though nothing tastes quite like fresh mayonnaise. Include on this list of "no nos" commercial jams and jellies, pickles, relishes, chutneys and such exotics as brandied or pickled peaches; they are too simple to make and taste far far better than the store-bought kind, to say nothing of the really substantial savings of being homemade. Cake, roll, biscuit, and corn bread mixes are a sin to the budget and to the table, and as for icing mixes, instant puddings, etc., I just won't mention them.

Finally, the most economical things you can buy are good pots, casseroles and saucepans. I like enameled cast iron that goes from stove top to oven without a qualm. Corning's ceramic glass casseroles and stew pots are a great addition to any kitchen. Needed, too, are shallow baking dishes and a soufflé mold, two or three really sharp knives and a cutting board. Add to this some good wooden spoons, a wire whisk, a spatula, a small hand-size electric mixer and, if possible, a good blender. These are economies? Yes, they are, for with a small initial investment you can turn inexpensive food into epicurean meals.

SMALL EXTRAVAGANCIES
(Well worth their price for adding interest and
flavor to low-cost cooking)

Sour cream: Used sparingly for desserts and sauces, a pint container will last for a week.

Whipping cream: The new sterilized type doesn't taste as good as the old-fashioned kind but it does keep, and a bit used where needed does add a luxurious touch.

Good quality coarsely ground black Java pepper: I like Spice Island brand the best. The cost per dish is infinitesimal and the taste difference is tremendous.

Worcestershire sauce: Lea & Perrins is my favorite and indispensable for adding flavor to any number of meat dishes.

Fresh parsley: Not an extravagance if you grow your own and not even too expensive if you select a really fresh bunch, rush it home and immediately wash in cold running water, wrap in a wet tea towel and store in the refrigerator until needed. It will stay crisp for a week.

Good quality natural cider vinegar: Again, the few pennies are well spent for added flavor.

Butter: I know this is hard to defend and you can, of course, substitute margarine in any recipe given in this book; but butter is butter and margarine is margarine, just like champagne is champagne and ginger ale is ginger ale. Used sparingly it adds the flavor only butter can give. Make sponge cake instead of a butter cake, serve fewer madeleines or cookies, but make them worth the trouble of making by using butter where called for.

Horseradish: A good brand of prepared horseradish is wonderful for zipping up the taste of so many foods. Keep well refrigerated.

Fresh lemon juice: The bottled variety is an offense against good cooking. Look for plump lemons when you buy and immerse them in boiling water, then roll them hard before cutting and squeezing—you'll get every drop of juice if you do.

Wines and spirits: Really great food is impossible without them, but they need not be the expensive imported variety; California wines and brandy serve equally well and a little goes a long way. I have purposely limited the amounts suggested in this book, and I believe you will find them well worth the small cost per serving.

You can get by nicely with the following:

California dry red wine—Gallo's Mountain Burgundy is fine. Buy the gallon size for extra savings.

California dry sherry—a fortified wine that keeps well after opening, so you can use the small amount called for and store the rest for future use.

California dry vermouth—use for any recipe calling for dry white wine. Again, this is a fortified wine so you can use just a little and reserve the rest for later. Or use a California dry white wine and serve a well-chilled glass of it with the meal.

California brandy—I can't cook without it. It lifts fresh fruit and simple desserts, like rice custard and bread pudding, out of the ordinary and into something special. Used for flaming various meat dishes, it adds unbelievable flavor to the least expensive cuts.

TO CUT THE COST OF COOKING

Stews: Use less meat, more vegetables. Make up for lost protein by using homemade stock. Oven brown the meat without expensive butter or oil. (see stew recipes for "how to")

Meat loaves: Use less meat, more bread crumbs. Make up for lost protein by using part wheat germ, adding an extra egg and using beef stock as liquid.

White sauce: Make white or cream sauce into sauce velouté by using clear, fat-free homemade chicken stock in place of milk or cream. It's ten times (or more) as good at one tenth the price.

Casseroles: Think before proceeding. Do you really need all the spices listed in the recipe? Unless you have them on hand, substitute or eliminate—you usually don't need that much seasoning. Don't spend money on a rarely used spice for an otherwise inexpensive dish.

Chicken: When the recipe says sauté the chicken pieces in oil or butter, DON'T. Oven sauté them in their own fat. (see page 84 for "how to")

Brown sauce or gravy for meats: Use fat-free beef stock, plus a bit of red wine. Bring to a boil, let simmer until reduced by half. Season with salt and pepper, if desired, then thicken with a little cornstarch mixed to a paste with a little water. No butter or flour is needed for this true gourmet sauce.

Fish: If you must fry, don't deep fat fry. Pan fry in a little oil or butter—it tastes better, and takes less expensive oil and shortening.

Learn the art and true pleasure of poaching. It's usually the least expensive as well as one of the most delicious ways to prepare your catch. (see page 102 for "how to")

Salad dressing: The best and least expensive is, of course, homemade and simple, just top quality oil and vinegar. I like about 5 parts oil to 1 part vinegar, plus a sprinkling of sugar, salt and pepper.

Make less, use less. A salad tastes best when all ingredients are very lightly coated, not swimming in dressing.

IF YOUR RECIPE CALLS FOR:

Chocolate: You can substitute 3 tbs. cocoa plus one tbs. butter or margarine.

2 egg yolks: You can use one whole egg.

Buttermilk: You can substitute whole sweet milk "soured" by stirring in 1 tbs. lemon juice or vinegar.

Chili sauce: You can use 1 cup homemade tomato sauce plus ½ cup brown sugar, 3 tbs. vinegar.

Milk: Substitute ½ cup evaporated milk plus ½ cup water or 1 cup nonfat milk solids plus 1 tsp. butter.

Budget sour cream: 1 cup cottage cheese, 2 tbs. lemon juice, a tsp. grated onion all whirled in electric blender until smooth. This can't be used in cooking but tastes great over fruit or vegetables or as an accompaniment.

chapter one

Basic Recipes to Save By

BASIC RECIPES
FOR THE THRIFTY COOK

To save money on food bills requires not so much self-denial or hours of work but knowledge of food. Basic knowledge of how to make stock, cook a pot roast, braise a ham, or bake a turkey can result in a whole repertoire of soups and main course dishes that utilize the built-in leftovers for maximum taste and minimum cost. Stock, of course, is not only essential for deep-down flavor to leftover cookery, real plan-ahead cooking, but for an almost endless number of great soups that are long on flavor and short on cost.

The next essential basic knowledge is about bread, hot rolls, coffee cake, cinnamon buns, cheese rolls. All can add interest and pleasure to low-cost budgets. They are so easy to make it becomes ridiculous to pay the price of bakery or freezer-shelf replicas, and that's just what they are, for nothing matches the flavor of the homemade variety.

Here are what I call the essentials:

Classic Beef and Chicken Stock
Classic Pot Roast

Classic Braised Ham
Roast Turkey or Chicken
Basic Rolls and Coffee Cake

STOCK

A million words and almost as many recipes have been written about stock, but surprisingly few people really make it and keep a supply on hand in either refrigerator or freezer; that's really too bad, for stock is the essential ingredient to fine cooking and no chef worth his salt would be without it. It is also virtually free, for stock is made largely from what we throw away.

Perhaps the reason for this is that most recipes for stock seem so complicated that in reading them over the average cook is appalled and rushes to the canned-soup counter for the easy way out. The truth is that stock is childishly simple to make, takes almost no work and little working time. True, it must simmer on the back of the stove for hours, but the cook doesn't have to simmer along with it; stock does well on its own.

Basically, all stock is made the same way, whether chicken or meat. The bones are simmered for hours in water with a bit of wine along with whatever seasonings are on hand. The wine is not so much for flavor but to release the natural gelatin of the bones which gives good stock its flavor and food value. The liquid is then strained and stored and the bones and seasoning vegetables are discarded. Not very complicated, is it? Now, to be specific, here are two easy recipes, one for meat and one for chicken. Either one is the base for dozens of fabulously good, easy soups, sauces and casseroles.

BEEF STOCK

1 veal knuckle bone
3 lbs. marrow bones (or if veal
   knuckle is not available
   use 4 lbs. marrow bones)
1 pig's foot (optional but very
   good)
3 onions, peeled
3 or 4 carrots, peeled and cut
   into 2-inch pieces
3 or 4 cloves garlic, peeled
Salt
Pepper
¼ cup dry red wine

Add any or all of the
   following:
celery tops
green pepper
leftover vegetables
any bones leftover from
   servings of any type of
   meat
parsley stems
end pieces of mushrooms
tomato peelings and end
   pieces

Place the bones in a large heavy soup kettle—about 4 or 5 quarts (I like the enameled cast iron ones best). Place in a moderate 350°F. oven and roast until bones are well browned, about 30 minutes. Turn once to assure even browning.

Remove kettle from oven and place on top of the stove. Add all remaining ingredients and fill kettle with water to 2 inches of rim. Bring to a boil over high heat; then immediately lower to a bare simmer. Simmer for at least 8 hours or longer, adding additional water (to come about 2 inches from rim of kettle) as needed. Stock may be turned off and left standing over night and reheated to simmer the following day. The stock is ready to strain when it takes on a slightly glazed appearance and has a robust, hearty taste. This is produced by the released gelatin. Some bones have more gelatin than others so if the stock seems thin allow it to cook down to about half for the desired result.

Cool and strain into a large bowl, discard bones and vegetables, if there is any soft marrow left in the bones push it out with the end of a spoon and add to stock. Place stock in refrigerator to chill until fat rises to the surface and hardens. Remove and discard fat and pour stock into 2-cup containers (I use well-washed empty cottage cheese containers) and refrigerate (up to one week) or freeze (up to one month).

The amount of stock depends on the marrow in the bones and how much you have to cook it down. If you use the pig's foot your stock will have sufficient bone marrow to reach the proper consistency with less boiling down.

To use frozen stock, place containers in a pan of cold water until sufficiently thawed to remove and use.

CHICKEN STOCK

This is even easier and, except for a few cents for vegetables, it costs nothing at all. Every time I serve chicken, I place the wings, back, neck and gizzard in a plastic bag and freeze. When the cooked chicken has been eaten the remaining bones go into the plastic bag. Sometimes I go ahead and make the stock the next day, or I may wait a week serve chicken again, add to my stockpile of bones and scrap pieces and make a double amount. It doesn't matter; it just depends on how much stock you want.

*Leftover pieces and bones from
    one or two chickens
2 onions, peeled and cut in
    half
2 carrots, scraped and cut in
    quarters
3 cloves garlic, peeled
2 tsps. salt
¼ cup white wine (you can
    use red if you have to)*

*Add any or all of the
    following:
1 bay leaf
celery tops
green pepper pieces
mushroom stems
peel and ends of tomatoes
parsley stems
an apple peeled, cored and
    cut in quarters
grated lemon peel
leftover lettuce leaves*

Place the chicken bones and pieces, vegetables and seasonings in a heavy 4- to 5-quart kettle (the enameled cast iron ones are best) and fill to within 2 inches of the rim with cold water. Bring to a boil over high heat and immediately lower heat to a slow simmer. Cook, barely simmering, for 3 to 4 hours adding more water if necessary to keep liquid about ¾ of the way up the kettle. Be cautious about adding water to chicken stock, though; it does not require the length of time to cook down as beef stock, and what you want is a hearty, robust flavor not hot water. Like beef stock the chicken stock is ready when it takes on a slightly glazed appearance that indicates the gelatin has been released from the bones. The stock is ready to be strained through a colander into a large bowl (push down on the vegetables to extract all the juices). Refrigerate until fat has risen to the surface and hardened. Remove and discard fat. If you have done a really good job your stock may have jellied by now and may have to be reheated a bit to liquify enough to be poured into 2-cup containers. Refrigerate for up to 1 week or freeze for up to 3 to 4 weeks.

Makes about 6 to 8 cups of stock

CLASSIC POT ROAST

This is a basic recipe that can be varied with equally delicious results by using 2 cups of beer for Beef Flamande. Either way the results are superb eating and wonderfully flavorful, moist leftovers—if such fare can be described as such.

¼ lb. salt pork
3 lbs. boneless chuck or
    bottom round of beef in
    one piece (whatever is the
    best buy at the moment)
Salt
Coarsely ground black pepper
2 tbs. butter
6 onions, peeled and sliced
3 cloves garlic, minced
2 tbs. flour

1 cup dry red wine and 1 cup
    of water (or 2 cups
    beer, dark if possible)
2 cups fat-free beef stock (see
    page 17)
1 tbs. sugar
1 tbs. vinegar
2 tsps. Spice Parisienne
3 tbs. parsley, finely chopped
    (optional)

Wash the salt pork under cold water to free it of excess salt. Pat dry. Cut into 1-inch cubes. In a heavy deep kettle (one that will go from stove top to oven; sauté the pork cubes over very low heat until they are crisp and all fat has been rendered. Remove the crisp cubes and set aside. Wipe the meat with a towel and sprinkle with salt and pepper. Heat the fat from the salt pork to almost smoking and brown the meat in it, turning once to brown evenly. Turn with two wooden spoons to avoid piercing the meat as this will cause the juice to run out and the meat will be dry and tough. When the meat is nicely browned remove to a platter and set aside. Pour off any remaining fat in the kettle and if necessary wipe out any burned bits that may have accumulated. Return the pot to the stove and add the butter. Melt over low heat, add onions and garlic and sauté until they are limp and golden. Stir in the flour and continue to cook over very low heat, stirring constantly, for 3 to 4 minutes, until it gives off a nutlike fragrant aroma. Slowly add the wine or beer, stirring constantly to blend into a smooth sauce; add the beef stock and stir to blend. Stir in sugar, vinegar, and Spice Parisienne.

Preheat oven to 350°F.

Next add the browned meat to the cooking liquid and bring to a boil over medium heat. Remove from heat, cover and place in preheated oven; bake for 1 to 1½ hours or until meat is tender. Remove meat to a platter and return kettle to the top of the stove. Bring liquid to a boil over medium heat, stirring constantly, for 5 to 10 minutes until liquid is reduced to a smooth sauce. Slice required servings from pot roast, cover with sauce and sprinkle with parsley if desired.

Serve with boiled or oven-roasted potatoes and carrots and onions Parisienne (winter); or fresh-cooked green beans (summer). Crusty French bread is essential to "mop up" the sauce, as is a glass of cold beer or dry red wine depending on which was used in the recipe.

Store leftover roast (don't slice) carefully in a deep glass storage dish, pour remaining sauce over meat, cover tightly and refrigerate until ready to use.

CLASSIC BRAISED HAM

Most of us American cooks tend to think of ham as baked ham and, while delicious it may be, braised ham is not only superior in taste and tenderness but it is far more economical. The meat does not shrink in the cooking as it does in baking and, being moister, it is much more desirable for use in subsequent dishes as well as being delicious the first time around. Look for a ham that is dry cured, that is *no* water added; the water-added variety, which is what most supermarkets sell, is puffed up with water to give the illusion of more meat for your money—what you are really paying for is meat *plus* water and with prices what they are no one needs to pay for *water*. The nonwatered variety are a bit more per pound, but you are only paying for meat and that's all you should pay for, so do read the label carefully before buying.

*½ ham, about 6 lbs. (the butt
    end provides more meat)*
3 tbs. butter
6 carrots, scraped
4 onions, peeled and minced
*4 or 5 stalks celery, coarsely
    chopped*

*2 cups unsweetened pineapple
    juice*
*6 cups clear, fat-free chicken
    stock (see page 18)*

Preheat oven to 325°F.

Remove the skin and all but about a ½-inch layer of fat from ham. Score the fat at 2-inch intervals in a crisscross pattern. Melt the butter over low heat in a deep, heavy kettle (enameled cast iron is best) that has a tight-fitting lid and that will go from stove top to oven. Add the vegetables and cook very slowly until vegetables begin to soften and turn golden in color. Remove from heat. Add ham, fat side up, and pour in pineapple juice and stock. Cover kettle and place in preheated oven. Cook for 1 hour, basting occasionally. Test ham for tenderness with the prongs of a fork. Do not allow to overcook or it will become stringy. Remove to a platter and let cool for about 30 minutes before slicing off desired serving portions.

An easy quick sauce can be made by melting 1 tbs. butter and stirring in 1 tbs. flour; cook 2 or 3 minutes over low heat, slowly adding 1 cup of strained braising liquid skimmed of surface fat. (This is easier if you place the 1 cup of liquid in the freezer for 10 to 15 minutes so that fat rises to the surface and hardens; then it can be easily removed and discarded). Stir mixture while adding liquid and cook, stirring contantly for 3 or 4 minutes until sauce is smooth and thick. Serve the ham and sauce with steamed quarters of fresh green cabbage and squares of hot corn bread.

Store leftover ham in a deep, heavy glass casserole with a tight-fitting lid. Pour strained braising liquid over meat, cover and refrigerate until ready to use.

Serves 8 to 10

ROAST TURKEY
WITH CALIFORNIA WALNUT STUFFING

Don't wait for Thanksgiving or Christmas for roast turkey. Pound for pound it is one of your best buys and not only very, very good right from the oven but a superb supply of leftover meat for any number of innovations.

To my mind there is only one way to roast a turkey and that is by what is known as the high heat method. It's a little, but not much, more trouble and the difference between a truly roasted bird and one that is more or less steamed is spectacular. If you are dubious about serving turkey except on Thanksgiving or at Christmas, try cold roast turkey with hot dressing, and a summer salad of fresh fruit. Add a glass of chilled white wine if you like and finish with madeleines and coffee.

1 10- to 11-lb. turkey (If
    frozen turkey is used,
    defrost in the refrigerator
    for 24 hours before
    cooking. I do not use the
    self-basting or butter-
    basted type of bird as
    these are not basted with
    real butter and, in my
    opinion, the flavor is
    ruined.)
6 tbs. butter, room
    temperature
6 thin slices salt pork
1 cup onion, minced
1 cup celery, minced
8 cups soft bread cubes
1 cup turkey liver and gizzard
    stock (Made by simmering
turkey gizzard in 2 cups
    of water to which you
    have added 1 chopped
    carrot and two peeled
    cloves of garlic for about
    45 minutes or until
    tender; add turkey livers
    last 15 minutes of
    cooking.)
2 eggs, lightly beaten
1 cooked turkey liver, finely
    chopped
1 cooked turkey gizzard, finely
    chopped
½ cup walnuts, chopped
1½ tsp. salt
1 tsp. coarsely ground black
    pepper
½ cup brandy

Preheat oven to 425°F.

Remove the gizzard and liver from the turkey; place in cold water and cook as directed above.

Rub turkey with 3 tbs. of the soft butter and place in a shallow roasting pan. Cover top of bird with the salt pork slices.

Melt remaining butter in a small skillet over low heat, add onions and celery and sauté until vegetables are soft and golden. Place bread cubes in a large mixing bowl, add sautéed vegetables and all remaining ingredients. Blend well. Stuff turkey lightly, leaving room for expansion while cooking. If there is any extra dressing, pour into greased loaf pan and re-frigerate until ready to bake in 300°F. oven for 20 to 25 minutes.

Place stuffed turkey in preheated oven and roast for 15 minutes. Lower heat to 350°F. and continue to roast, basting occasionally with the drippings. Roast for 20 to 25 minutes to the pound. If bird seems too dry, add about ¼ cup water to the pan and continue to baste every 15 to 20 minutes. The turkey is done when the leg joint will move easily up and down and the surface is golden brown.

Remove from heat and let rest for 20 to 25 minutes before carving into serving slices.

Cut leftover turkey from the bone, carefully wrap meal-size portions in freezer paper and seal before freezing. Or refrigerate, covered, for up to 1 week.

Serves 10 to 12

ROLLS OR COFFEE CAKE
TO BAKE NOW OR FREEZE FOR LATER

This is a new "specially" easy recipe that cuts down the time needed for rising.

Basic Dough

5 ½ to 6 ½ cups all-purpose
     flour, unsifted
½ cup sugar
1 ½ tsp. salt
2 packages active dry yeast

1 ¼ cups water
½ cup milk
¼ lb. butter
2 eggs, room temperature

In a large bowl thoroughly mix 2 cups of the flour, sugar, salt, and yeast. Combine water, milk, and butter in a saucepan. Heat over low heat until liquids are very warm (120° to 130°F.). Gradually add to dry ingredients and beat at medium speed of electric mixer for 2 minutes, scraping bowl occasionally. Add eggs and ½ cup flour. Beat at high speed for 2 minutes, scraping bowl occasionally. Stir in enough additional flour to make a soft dough. Turn out onto a lightly floured board; knead until smooth and elastic, about 8 to 10 minutes. Cover with a damp towel, let rest in a warm place for 20 minutes or until doubled in bulk.

Rolls to freeze for later

Punch dough down. Shape into small balls and place on greased baking sheets. Freeze until firm, then transfer to freezer bags. Freeze for up to 4 weeks.

Remove from freezer; place on greased baking sheets. Cover and let rise in a warm place free from draft until doubled in bulk, about 1½ hours.

Bake at 350°F. for 15 minutes, or until golden brown and done. Remove from baking sheets and cool on wire racks.

Rolls to bake now

Punch dough down. Shape into small balls. Place on greased baking sheets and let rise until doubled in bulk. Bake in a preheated 350°F. oven until lightly browned.

Apple coffee cake for now

Prepare basic dough. Punch down and divide in half. Roll out one half of dough. Sprinkle with ½ cup brown sugar, ½ cup finely chopped, peeled, seeded and cored tart apples. Roll up. Place seam side down on a greased cookie sheet. Repeat with second half of dough. Cover and let stand until doubled in bulk. Bake in a preheated 350°F. oven until lightly browned, about 30 minutes. Cool slightly before slicing.

Cranberry bread for now

½ cup fresh or frozen cranberries	1 tsp. lemon rind, grated
¼ cup water	½ cup sugar
	Basic Dough

Place cranberries, water, lemon rind and sugar in a saucepan. Cook, stirring, over low heat until sugar is dissolved, cranberries are soft and syrup has thickened.

Prepare basic dough. Punch down and divide in half. Roll out one half, spread with half of the cranberry mixture. Roll up and place seam side down on a greased cookie sheet. Repeat with remaining dough. Cover and let rise in a warm place until doubled in bulk. Bake in a preheated 350°F. oven until lightly browned, about 30 minutes.

chapter two

Soup, Beautiful, Thrifty Soup

SOUP OF THE DAY

Soup is the most sadly neglected dish in the cook's repertoire, yet soup, really good soup, can save the budget and please even the most finicky gourmet. Homemade soups made with stock, milk or beans are top quality protein and sound nutrition, but more important they are superb eating. If your idea of homemade soup is the greasy vegetable variety of your childhood (It was mine for too many years), forget it. I'm talking about such soups as delicate cucumber, satisfying black bean with sherry, real French onion—all marvelous on a cold winter night; or ice cold vichysoisse served for a summer day luncheon.

Soup is easy on the cook as well as the pocketbook. All included here can be made mostly in minutes and even those that require a bit of cooking do not require constant attendance. Needless to say, almost all can be made ahead and reheated or chilled until ready to serve. Best of all, a menu built around a really good nutritious soup can be extra simple yet extra good. Try a few of the menus outlined here. I don't think you'll have any complaints.

SIX WINTER SOUP MENUS
FOR LUNCHEON, DINNER OR SUPPER

(asterisk indicates recipe to be found in this book)

BLACK BEAN SOUP *
PUMPERNICKEL BREAD AND BUTTER
SPINACH SALAD WITH PORK BITS *
DEEP DISH APPLE PIE
WITH CRUMB TOPPING

FRENCH ONION SOUP *
CRUSTY FRENCH BREAD AND BUTTER
BEAN AND CELERY SALAD
BANANAS FLAMBÉ *

CORN CHOWDER *
HOT CORN STICKS
APPLE AND CABBAGE COLESLAW *
AMBROSIA *

LENTIL SOUP *
HOT GARLIC FRENCH BREAD
ORANGE AND PURPLE ONION SALAD
COFFEE-CAN APPLE PUDDING

CREAM OF SQUASH SOUP
WITH OYSTERS *
OYSTER CRACKERS
GAZPACHO SALAD *
APPLESAUCE CAKE *
WITH CREAM CHEESE TOPPING

POTAGE GARBURE PAYSANNE *
HOT GARLIC FRENCH BREAD
COMPOTE OF WINTER FRUITS
IN BRANDY
"ANYTHING GOES" COOKIES *

SIX SUMMER SOUP MENUS
FOR LUNCHEON, DINNER OR SUPPER

VICHYSSOISE *
ITALIAN BREAD STICKS
TEXAS TOMATO SALAD *
DEEP-DISH PEACH PIE *

SEAFOOD BISQUE *
HEATED FRENCH BREAD
SUMMER FRUIT BOWL
"ANYTHING GOES" COOKIES *

CREAM OF CUCUMBER SOUP *
ITALIAN BREAD STICKS
CORN SALAD *
MELON BALLS SPRINKLED WITH POWDERED
SUGAR AND CHOPPED MINT

CREAM OF TOMATO SOUP *
SALTINES
HOMEGROWN LETTUCE SALAD
WITH POPPY SEED DRESSING *
SPONGE CAKE * WITH FRESH PEACHES

MELON SLICES WITH THIN-SLICED SALAMI
AND BLACK BREAD AND BUTTER
MACARONI SOUP *
FIGS AND PEACHES IN RED WINE

JELLIED CHICKEN CONSOMMÉ
WITH CURRIED MAYONNAISE *
SPICY POTTED HAM SPREAD SANDWICHES *
SUMMER FRUIT SALAD
WITH POPPY SEED DRESSING *

FRENCH ONION SOUP

2 tbs. butter
1 lb. Bermuda onions, peeled
     and very thinly sliced
1 clove garlic
1½ qts. fat-free chicken stock
     (see page 18)
Beurre manié of 1 tbs. soft
     butter kneaded into 2 tsp.
     flour to form a smooth
     mixture

Salt
Freshly ground black pepper
6 1-inch thick slices French
     bread
2 tbs. olive oil
2 tbs. Parmesan cheese, grated

Accompaniments
French bread
Grated Parmesan cheese

Melt the butter in a heavy, 5- to 6-quart enamel or stainless steel pot. Add the onions and cook over low heat, stirring occasionally, for 20 to 30 minutes or until they are very soft and a light golden color. Don't allow them to burn as this will give the soup an unpleasant flavor.

Pour in the stock, bring to a boil and then reduce heat to its lowest possible point.

Peel the garlic, split it in half lengthwise, stick a colored food pick in one half and add it to the pot. Reserve remaining half clove.

Partially cover the pot and let the soup simmer very gently for 30 to 40 minutes. Remove and discard garlic. Stir in beuree manié and continue to stir until thick and smooth.

While the soup is simmering prepare the French bread.

Preheat oven to 325°F.

Arrange the bread slices side by side on a baking sheet.

Place in the preheated oven for about 10 minutes. Brush both sides of each slice with olive oil (using a total of 1 tbs. of the oil) and rub each with the remaining half clove of garlic. Continue to bake until crisp and light golden in color. Set aside.

When ready to serve preheat the oven to 375°F.

Ladle the soup into deep individual oven-proof bowls, top each with a slice of the toasted bread and sprinkle evenly with the 2 tbs. cheese and the remaining olive oil. Bake for 10 to 15 minutes or until cheese has melted.

Serve at once with additional grated Parmesan cheese and crusty French bread to pass at the table.

Notes:

The soup can be made ahead and reheated. The flavor improves for "standing." The toast can, of course, also be made ahead.

VICHYSSOISE

Easy and elegant, there's nothing more delicious on a warm day. Because it is made with homemade chicken stock and milk it is not only superb eating but superb nutrition as well. This summer recipe uses readily available fresh green onions instead of leeks for an even fresher flavor and lower cost.

1 bunch fresh green onions (nonwilted tops)	2 cups clear, fat-free chicken stock (see page 18)
2 tbs. butter	1 cup water
3 medium-size potatoes, peeled and cut into small pieces	½ tsp. salt
	2 cups milk

Chop white part of onions. Reserve green tops. Heat butter in a generous-size saucepan and sauté onions until limp. Add potatoes, stock, water and salt. Bring to a boil, then lower heat to simmering and cook until potatoes are very soft. Remove from heat and purée in a blender, being careful not to fill the blender more than half full. Return the soup to the saucepan and add milk; bring to a boil, then remove from heat. Check seasoning for salt. Chill thoroughly. Chop onion tops very finely and sprinkle over soup just before serving.

Serves 6

CREAM OF TOMATO SOUP

2 large summer-ripe tomatoes
1 small bunch green onions (homegrown, I hope) or 1 small white onion
1 tbs. butter

2 cups strong homemade chicken stock (see page 18)
Salt
Pepper
1 tsp. fresh basil, chopped (optional)
2 cups milk

Peel the tomatoes by immersing in boiling water for a moment and then slipping off the skins. Chop the white part only of the green onions, reserving the tops, or peel and mince whole onion. Melt the butter in a 2-quart saucepan and sauté the onion until limp and golden. Chop the tomatoes into the onions and cook over very low heat until the tomatoes are almost liquid. (Chop with the tip of a spatula as they cook.) Add chicken stock and cook over low heat for 15 to 20 minutes. Season to taste, add milk and heat until steamy hot. Chop green tops of onions very finely and sprinkle over surface before serving.

Serves 4 to 6

CREAM OF CUCUMBER SOUP

2 medium-size cucumbers
3 cups chicken stock (see page 18)
2 tbs. butter
2 tbs. flour

1 cup milk
Salt
Pepper
Croutons

Peel cucumbers, cut in half lengthwise, scoop out seeds and then chop each half.

Place in a saucepan and add 2 cups of the stock. Bring to a boil, then lower heat and let simmer until cucumber is tender, about 20 minutes. Transfer to an electric blender and blend until smooth, or force through a sieve. Set aside.

Melt the butter in a heavy pot and stir in the flour. When smooth, blend in the cucumber mixture, the remaining stock and the milk. Season with salt and pepper and heat until steamy hot.

Serve garnished with croutons.

Serves 4 to 6

JELLIED CHICKEN CONSOMMÉ WITH CURRIED MAYONNAISE

3 cups homemade strong, clear chicken stock (see page 18)
1 envelope unflavored gelatin

Salt, if needed
4 tsp. mayonnaise
1 tsp. curry powder

This recipe works only if your chicken stock is the strong homemade variety that jells almost by itself.

Heat the chicken stock to boiling, dissolve the gelatin in a small amount of cold water in a large mixing bowl. Pour boiling stock over gelatin and stir until dissolved. Check for seasoning and place in refrigerator until firm and set. Blend curry powder into mayonnaise. Break up firm consommé with a fork. Pile into soup cups. Garnish each serving with a teaspoon of curry mayonnaise and serve ice cold.

Serves 4

POTAGE GARBURE PAYSANNE
(Thick Vegetable Soup)

3 stalks celery, finely chopped
1 onion, peeled and finely
    chopped
1 white turnip, peeled and
    finely chopped
2 tbs. butter
½ cup water
5 cups chicken stock (see page

18) or half stock and half
    water
Salt
Pepper
4 or 6 slices of French bread
Butter, room temperature
Parmesan cheese, grated

Cook the vegetables in the butter in a soup pot over very low heat for 5 minutes, stirring constantly. Add water, cover and let steam until they are soft, stirring frequently, about 30 minutes. Add the stock and let simmer very gently for 1 hour.

Force the soup through a fine sieve or purée in electric blender. Season with salt and pepper. Reheat until steamy hot.

Toast the French bread lightly, spread with soft butter and sprinkle with grated cheese. Place a slice of this toast in each soup bowl. Pour soup over and serve at once.

Serves 4 to 6

CREAM OF SQUASH SOUP WITH OYSTERS

Oysters are expensive but, if you love oysters as I do, here's a way to make a few go a long way.

3 large acorn (Hubbard)
    squash
Water
4 cups milk
1 tbs. butter

2 tbs. onion, minced
1 pt. oysters with liquid
Salt
Pepper

Cut squash in quarters lengthwise. Peel each quarter and remove seeds. Place in a saucepan and add about 1 cup water.

Cover and steam until very soft. Drain and place in electric blender with 1 cup of the milk. Blend until smooth.

Melt butter in a large, heavy pot over low heat; add onion and sauté until limp. Then add puréed squash and remaining milk and cook, stirring, over very low heat until smooth and thick. Add oysters and season with salt and pepper. Heat until edges of oysters curl.

Serve very hot with unsalted crackers.

Serves 6 to 8

SEAFOOD BISQUE

1 tbs. butter
1 small tart apple, peeled, seeded, cored and very finely minced
1 small white onion, peeled and very finely minced
1 to 2 tsps. curry powder
2½ cups boiling hot fish stock (see pages 102 and 103)

1 large California white potato, peeled and chopped
½ lb. fresh fillet of sole cut into narrow strips
1½ cups milk
¼ cup dry sherry
Salt
Pepper

Melt butter in soup pot over low heat; add apple and onion and cook, stirring often for 10 to 15 minutes. Stir in curry powder. Add hot stock and chopped potato. Stir to blend. Bring to a boil, then lower heat and let simmer until potato is soft, about 25 minutes. Add fish strips. Continue to simmer until they are firm and white. Add milk and sherry. Taste, season with salt and pepper and heat to steaming, but do not allow to boil. Serve very hot with unsalted soda crackers.

Serves 4 to 6

LENTIL SOUP

2 cups dried lentils

3 qts. water

1 meaty ham bone

1 onion, peeled and quartered

Salt

Pepper

½ cup milk

In a soup pot put lentils, water, ham bone and onion. Bring to a boil, then lower heat and let simmer about 2 hours until lentils are very tender. Remove and discard ham bone. Ladle about 3 cups of lentils and a little of the liquid into container of electric blender. Blend until smooth and return this purée back to the soup pot. Season with salt and pepper. Stir in milk. Heat to steaming.

Serve very hot with crusty French bread.

Serves 8 to 10

CORN CHOWDER

1 tbs. butter

1 small onion, peeled and
    minced

2 cups clear, fat-free chicken
    stock (see page 18); or use
    1 cup stock, 1 cup water

1 large California white
    potato, peeled and
    chopped

1 1-lb. can cream-style corn

Salt

Freshly ground black pepper

Dash tabasco sauce

Milk, if desired

Minced parsley

In soup pot melt butter over low heat. Add onion and sauté until limp; add stock (or stock and water) and potato. Let simmer until potato is tender.

With a slotted spoon remove about ½ of the potato cubes. Place in electric blender with about 1 cup of the stock. Blend until smooth and return mixture to soup pot. Stir in corn. Season with salt, pepper and tabasco, and add additional stock, water or milk to thin consistency, if necessary. (But the chowder should be quite thick.)

Serve very hot with unsalted soda crackers.

Serves 4 to 6

MACARONI SOUP

This is a hearty soup with an Italian flavor that makes good use of homemade beef stock.

2 tbs. butter
1 small onion, peeled and minced
1 clove garlic, peeled and minced
2 tomatoes, peeled, seeded and chopped
4 cups homemade beef stock (see page 17)

1 cup water
1 tbs. tomato paste
½ tsp. Italian seasoning
1 8-oz. package elbow macaroni
Parmesan cheese (optional)

Melt the butter in a good-size saucepan. Add onion and garlic and sauté over low heat until limp. Add chopped tomatoes and continue to cook until tomatoes are soft, breaking them up with the tip of a spatula as they cook. Add stock, water, tomato paste and seasoning. Cook simmering over medium heat for 10 to 15 minutes. Recipe may be made ahead to this point. Bring to a full boil and add macaroni a little at a time to keep soup boiling. Boil for 5 to 10 minutes or until macaroni is just tender—*al dente*. Serve at once. Sprinkle each serving with Parmesan cheese, if desired.

Serves 6

BLACK BEAN SOUP

1 lb. dried black beans
1 large onion, peeled and
    chopped
6 or 8 leafy celery tops
Ham bone from baked ham
    with bits and pieces of
    leftover meat

Water, as needed
Salt, if needed
Coarsely ground black pepper
Dry sherry (room
    temperature)

Place beans in a colander and wash under cold water until the water runs clear.

Bring 2½ qts. water to a full boil in a heavy 4- to 5-qt. pot. Add the beans, onion, celery and ham bone. Let water return to boil; then lower heat, partially cover the pot and let simmer for about 3 hours or until the beans are sufficiently soft to mash easily with a spoon. Remove and discard ham bone; then using a large, heavy wooden spoon, force the soup through a colander set over a large bowl. Cover the bowl and refrigerate several hours (or overnight). Remove and discard congealed fat.

Return soup to pot and add about 1 cup of water, and stir until blended. Place over very low heat until bubbly hot. Taste, add salt if needed and pepper to taste. Ladle into deep soup bowls and immediately stir 1 to 2 tablespoons of dry sherry into each serving. Serve at once.

Serves 8 to 10

Notes

If desired, substitute red wine vinegar for the sherry. It's a different taste but also very good; but instead of stirring it into each serving, simply add about 2 tbs. (total amount) into the hot soup and cook a final five minutes.

chapter three

Main Course Meat Dishes

Meat is, after all, the favorite main course, especially for dinner, but meat is expensive, expensive, expensive. What to do? The answer of course is the thrifty cook's rule of three:

- Make a little meat go a long way.
- Learn the gourmet's way to cook less expensive cuts of meat.
- Broaden your cooking horizon with recipes from around the globe.

This is what I have done in this chapter, though certainly there are many other recipes for inexpensive meat dishes. Every one of the recipes here tastes wonderfully good and I don't think anyone will guess that each one was planned to pare down the butcher's bill.

I do have one additional suggestion that has proved helpful to me to save on meat and that is to find a reliable butcher, one you like and can trust. Supermarkets rarely have really good, less expensive, cuts of meat and never seem to have bones. A good butcher may be a few cents higher per pound, but in the long run you will save money as well as gain in variety and flavor.

These are all fairly substantial, almost one course dinners needing for the most part, only the addition of a salad or fruit dessert and in some instances a special bread. Nearly all of them make use of inexpensive cuts of meat and/or make a little meat go a long way. But the main point here is they are true epicurean fare. They are planned for good eating as well as to save money, for there is little point in preparing an inexpensive meal if everyone leaves the table feeling deprived. I hope they prove my point that thrifty cooking is good cooking, and I do believe that you will find they are just that-superb eating and economical. Here are a few suggestions for menus that I have found enjoyable and hope you will too.

SUMMER

(asterisk indicates recipe to be found in this book)

TEXAS BARBECUED SHANK OF BEEF
AND SKILLET CORN BREAD *
TEXAS TOMATO SALAD *
COLD BEER
COLD WATERMELON

LATIN MIXED MEAT
AND VEGETABLE STEW *
CRUSTY HARD ROLLS
COLD BEER
COLD BLUEBERRIES
WITH PEACH PURÉE *
COFFEE

DEVILED KIDNEYS *
CORN PUDDING *
CHILLED WHITE WINE
LEMON-CHEESE MOUSSE
COFFEE

FRESH TOMATO-CUCUMBER SHRUB *
STIR-FRIED PORK
WITH FRESH GREEN PEPPERS *
FRIDAY NIGHT PIE *

COLD MEAT LOAF
BREAD AND BUTTER PICKLES *
HORSERADISH
HOT MUSTARD
FRENCH POTATO SALAD *
COLD BEER
MIXED SUMMER FRUIT COMPOTE *

PORCH BUFFET SUPPER

MOUSSAKA *
CORN PUDDING *
CRUSTY FRENCH OR ITALIAN BREAD
CHILLED WHITE WINE
BLUEBERRIES AND SOUR CREAM
"ANYTHING GOES" COOKIES *

WINTER

IRISH STEW *
(PLENTY OF IT)
IRISH BEER
INDIAN PUDDING *
BASKET OF FRESH TANGERINES
COFFEE

MARINATED SHORT RIBS OF BEEF *
ROASTED POTATOES
APPLE AND CABBAGE COLESLAW *
COLD BEER
AMBROSIA *
COFFEE

SWEET AND SOUR CABBAGE
WITH FRANKFURTERS *
HOT MUSTARD
STUFFED BAKED POTATO *
COLD BEER
APPLE BETTY *

STUFFED GREEN PEPPERS *
MASHED TURNIPS *
DRY RED WINE
APPLESAUCE CAKE *
COFFEE

CREOLE KIDNEY STEW *
FRESHLY COOKED RICE
DRY RED WINE
ORANGE SLICES
WITH BROWN SUGAR AND SOUR CREAM
MADELEINES *
COFFEE

GROUND BEEF PAPRIKA
WITH FLAT NOODLES *
DRY RED WINE
ORANGE AND ONION SALAD
WITH PIQUANT DRESSING *
SWEET POTATO PONE *
WITH WHIPPED CREAM

MARINATED MEATS

Marinating is a centuries-old process for tenderizing tough cuts of meat and for adding superb flavor at the same time. Nothing could be easier: mix up the marinade in a large (nonmetal) bowl, put in the meat, cover and refrigerate for 24 to 36 hours. The only other thing you have to do is turn it a few times so the marinade is absorbed evenly by the meat. Inexpensive cuts of meat can be epicurean fare when they are marinated before cooking. Try . . .

MARINATED SHORT RIBS OF BEEF

1 tbs. hot mustard
3 tsp. salt
2 tsp. coarsely ground black
   pepper
1 tbs. chili powder
1 tbs. sugar
1 clove garlic, minced

½ cup cider vinegar
1 cup dry red wine
½ cup salad oil
2 lbs. short ribs cut into
   serving pieces
4 purple onions, peeled and
   cut into thick slices

Combine all ingredients except short ribs and purple onions in large (nonmetal) bowl, beat well with a wire whisk to blend. Add short ribs and turn to coat meat thoroughly with marinade. Cover and refrigerate for 24 to 36 hours, turning occasionally.

Preheat oven to 350°F.

Remove short ribs from marinade and place in a shallow roasting pan. Reserve marinade. Roast in preheated oven for 25 to 30 minutes or until brown. Remove from oven and lower heat to 300°F. Place onion slices between pieces of short ribs. Pour remaining marinade over meat and onions. Cover and bake 10 to 15 minutes longer until onions are brown and the fat on the ribs is crisp.

Serve with oven-roasted potatoes and coleslaw.

Serves 6

MARINATED BEEF À LA MODE

1 onion, peeled and chopped
1 carrot, scraped and cut in
    thin slices
3 cloves garlic, peeled and
    finely minced
2 tbs. chopped parsley, if
    available
3 tsp. salt
1 tsp. coarsely ground black
    pepper

1 tbs. sugar
1 tsp. Spice Parisienne
1 ½-inch piece green ginger,
    crushed
1 cup dry red wine
½ cup salad oil
4 lbs. shank of beef—large
    meaty slices with small
    bone
¼ lb. salt pork

Combine all ingredients except beef and salt pork in a large (nonmetal) bowl. Add beef shanks and turn to coat evenly with marinade. Cover and refrigerate 24 to 36 hours.

Wash salt pork under cold running water to remove excess salt, pat dry and cut into small cubes. In a deep, top-of-the-stove-to-oven casserole, sauté the pork cubes over low heat until crisp and all fat has been rendered. Remove cubes and drain on absorbent paper. (A brown paper bag from the grocery does nicely.) Remove beef shanks from the marinade, drain and pat dry. Reserve marinade. Heat the rendered fat to almost smoking and brown the beef shanks in it, turning once to brown evenly. Remove from heat and add reserved marinade, stirring to distribute marinade evenly.

Preheat oven to 300°F.

Cover meat and bake for 1½ hours, turning once or twice. Uncover and bake a final 10 minutes before serving. Serve with marinade as gravy. Sprinkle each serving with crisp pork bits and serve with heated, crusty French bread and, of course, a glass of dry red wine.

Serves 8

LATIN MIXED MEAT
AND VEGETABLE STEW

1 lb. beef chuck cut into 1-inch cubes
½ lb. lean boneless pork cut into 1-inch cubes
1 small ham bone from leftover braised or baked ham (optional)
2 cloves garlic, peeled
1 small chili pepper, split and seeded (optional)
4 to 6½ by 1-inch strips lemon peel
4 cups combined beef stock and water (or all stock)

4 medium-size potatoes, peeled and cut into 2-inch cubes
4 to 6 medium-size yellow squash cut into 1½-inch slices
1 lb. choriz (Spanish-style sausage)
2 plantains or under ripe bananas, peeled and sliced
Salt
Pepper

Put the beef, pork, ham bone (if you have one), garlic, chili pepper, lemon peel, and combined stock and water (or stock) in a stew pot. Bring to a boil, lower heat and let simmer for 1½ hours.

Remove and discard ham bone, garlic, chili pepper and lemon peel. Add potatoes and squash. Cover and cook until vegetables and meats are tender.

Meanwhile, prick choriz in several places with a small sharp knife. Place in a small skillet and cover with water. Let simmer for about 10 minutes. Drain and slice. Add to stew last 20 minutes of cooking. Add plantain or banana slices. Cover and cook a final 10 minutes.

Serves 6 to 8

Notes

Now this is a hearty stew, rich and filling. The changes you can make are many: use all pork or all beef if you prefer it to the combined meats; skip the ham bone unless you have it on hand. Instead of the chili pepper used in the stew base, add a few drops of hot chili sauce to the cooked stew just before serving. If yellow squash is out of season, use an equal amount of peeled and seeded chopped pumpkin—it's delicious and makes a great early fall dish. Also you don't need the plantain or bananas, though they do add something special, and I think you will like them.

OXTAIL RAGOUT

In this recipe the meat is oven browned in its own fat, eliminating the need to use expensive oil for browning. The flavor of the beef fat is superior and, of course, you save the price of the oil. This is another of what I call "loose" recipes—ones in which you can substitute ingredients or use less of one and more of another. The lemon peel gives an added dimension of flavor and it's free if you saved it by storing it in your freezer after squeezing the juice.

To extend servings add additional carrot chunks and little white onions the last 45 minutes of baking or serve with steamed new potatoes, pasta or rice. All are equally good.

4 lbs. oxtails cut into 1½-inch thick slices
4 to 6 celery stalks, chopped
1 large onion, peeled and chopped
2 cloves garlic, peeled and minced
1 carrot, scraped and chopped
1 tbs. flour
1 pig's foot, split (optional but it adds superb flavor)
8 cups water
½ cup dry red wine
2 tbs. red wine vinegar

1 tbs. sugar
½ tsp. salt
1 1-lb. can tomatoes, (or if in season use 1 lb. fresh tomatoes, chopped)
4 to 6 ½-inch strips of lemon peel
Salt
Pepper
Plus, if you have it, ¼ cup Madeira or brandy
(1 tbs. butter, 1 tbs. flour, if desired, to thicken stock)

Preheat oven to 350°F.

Place the oxtails in a large, heavy oven-to-stove pot in pre-heated oven until nicely browned, about 30 minutes. Remove pot from oven. Remove oxtails and set aside.

Add the celery, onion, garlic, and carrot to the rendered fat in the pot and cook over low heat, stirring frequently for about 10 minutes. Sprinkle with the flour; when it starts to brown, add a little of the water and stir until blended. Add the remaining water, wine, vinegar, sugar, salt and tomatoes. Stir to blend and return the oxtails to the pot. Add pig's foot. Cover and simmer over very low heat until the meat is sufficiently tender to pull from the bone, 2½ to 3 hours.

Remove oxtails and pig's foot. Set aside. Strain stock into a large bowl, pressing down on vegetables to extract all juice. Add meat to strained stock. Cover bowl and refrigerate until all fat has risen to surface; then remove and discard fat.

Pour strained stock into cooking pot. Cut oxtails into bite-size pieces and add to stock with pig's foot, if desired. Reheat to steamy hot. Season with salt and pepper and, if desired (or you have it), add Madeira or brandy.

If you want a thicker sauce, melt 1 tbs. of butter in a small skillet and stir in 1 tbs. of flour. Cook over low heat until mixture begins to brown and develops a nutlike fragrance. Add a little of the hot stock, blend and pour into the stew pot. Cook, stirring, the ragout a few minutes longer until sauce thickens.

Serves 8 or more (depending on the addition of carrots and onions).

A SUPER-TASTING, QUICK, EASY
AND INEXPENSIVE ROAST BEEF HASH

4 medium-large California
    white all-purpose
    potatoes
1 cup leftover lean pot roast of
    beef, finely chopped
2 tbs. vegetable shortening
½ tsp. salt

¼ tsp. pepper
2 tbs. butter
1 tsp. Worcestershire sauce
1 tbs. green onion tops, finely
    minced
4 tbs. sour cream

Adjust broiler rack to about 6 inches under heat. Preheat broiler.

Peel and shred potatoes, add to chopped beef and toss with a fork to blend.

Heat the shortening in a large skillet (with heat-proof handle) over medium heat. Sprinkle potato mixture evenly over entire surface of skillet. Don't pack down. Sprinkle with salt and pepper. Cook, without stirring, until underside is lightly browned. (Lift up edge with a spatula.) Melt butter and pour over surface. Place skillet under broiler heat until surface is browned. Turn out onto a warm plate. Mix Worcestershire into sour cream and spoon over surface. Sprinkle with minced green onion and serve at once.

Serves 4

BEEF AND KIDNEY PIE

This is a hearty main dish for 8 that makes a little meat go a very long way deliciously!

¼ lb. salt pork
4 lamb kidneys cut into cubes,
  skin and fat removed
1 lb. beef chuck cut into ½-
  inch cubes
1 tbs. butter
1 cup onion, minced
¼ cup green pepper, minced
2 cloves garlic, minced
1½ cups homemade beef stock
  (see page 17)
½ cup dry red wine

½ tsp. salt
1 tsp. coarsely ground black
  pepper
1 tbs. Worcestershire sauce
8 small white onions, peeled,
  and boiled to just tender
2 tbs. butter
2 tbs. flour
8 uncooked baking powder
  biscuits (see page 205)
Chopped parsley, if available

Wash pork in cold water to remove excess salt, dry and dice. Place pork in a heavy saucepan and cook over low heat until all fat has been rendered and pork cubes are crisp. Remove cubes and set aside. Heat fat in pan to almost smoking and brown kidneys and meat a few pieces at a time, removing them to a deep 2-quart casserole as they are browned. If the remaining fat in the pan appears burned, discard and wipe out pan before proceeding. If this is the case, increase the butter to 2 tbs. and melt in saucepan over low heat. Add onions, green pepper and garlic and sauté until vegetables are limp. Add beef stock and wine and heat to simmering. Cook, simmering, for about 15 minutes. In a small skillet melt the second 2 tbs. of butter, stir in the flour and cook, stirring constantly, over low heat for about 5 minutes. Remove from heat and add about 3 tbs. of the hot stock and wine mixture and mix to a smooth thick consistency. Pour back into wine-stock mixture. Add seasoning and Worcestershire sauce and blend. Add cooked onions to meat in casserole and pour sauce over both. Bake in 350°F. oven for 1 hour. Remove from oven and increase oven heat to 450°F. Place uncooked biscuits on top of meat and sauce, return to oven and bake for 10 to 15 minutes until biscuits have risen and are a golden brown. Serve very hot with 1 biscuit to each serving. Sprinkle each serving with parsley if desired.

Serves 8

TEXAS BARBECUED SHANK OF BEEF
AND SKILLET CORN BREAD

At this writing, shanks of beef are the least expensive beef at my market. It's been so for some time—and well it should be; this meat is tough, and most people still don't know that tough meat is often the most flavorful you can buy at any price. It takes a bit more cooking, but it's good, honest, meaty beef and nothing takes its place when that's what's wanted.

3 lbs. shank of beef
2 large onions, peeled and
    chopped
1 clove garlic, peeled and
    chopped
1 tsp. salt
½ tsp. coarsely ground black
    pepper
4 cups water (more if needed)

1 1-lb. can tomatoes
½ cup chili sauce
2 tbs. brown sugar
⅓ cup cider vinegar
1 tbs. Worcestershire sauce
1 tbs. chili powder
Skillet Corn Bread (recipe
    follows)

Preheat oven to 350°F.

Place the beef in a large, heavy stew pot in the preheated oven until browned, about 30 minutes. Turn it once or twice to insure even browning.

Place the pot on top of the stove and add the onions, garlic, salt, pepper and water. Bring to a boil; then lower heat and let simmer for 2½ hours. Add remaining ingredients and let simmer a final hour or until meat is very tender. Add additional water if sauce becomes too thick while cooking. Remove meat to a platter and cut into bite-size pieces. Return to pot and reheat briefly before spooning over hot-from-the-oven squares of fragrant skillet corn bread.

Serves 6 to 8

SKILLET CORN BREAD

This is best when made in a well-seasoned cast iron skillet, but a heavy enameled skillet will substitute nicely.

1 cup yellow cornmeal	*1½ cups milk*
½ cup flour	*1 tbs. cider vinegar*
1 tsp. salt	*3 tbs. vegetable shortening*
½ tsp. soda	*1 tbs. butter*
1 tsp. baking powder	*1 egg*

Preheat oven to 400°F.

Combine cornmeal, flour, salt, soda, and baking powder in a large mixing bowl and stir until well blended.

Mix milk with vinegar.

Put the shortening and butter in a heavy 9- to 10-inch skillet and place in the preheated oven until melted and hot.

Now—Work quickly!

Make a well in the center of the dry mixture and drop in the egg. Add the milk mixture and stir rapidly—don't worry about lumps—until blended. Pour in hot shortening and butter. Stir again, but quickly pour mixture into the hot skillet and place immediately in the oven. Bake 20 to 25 minutes or until firm and lightly browned on top.

To serve, cut from the pan into wedges.

Serves 6 to 8

BOEUF HACHE MADAME JEANNE

This is so good it can replace the most expensive steak even if you serve it as the main course for a dinner party.

For the beef
4 tbs. butter
¼ cup onion, minced
2 tbs. brandy
½ cup cold water
¾ tsp. salt
¼ tsp. coarsely ground black
pepper
1 tbs. Worcestershire sauce
1 lb. lean ground beef
1 tsp. mustard (see page 178)

½ cup soft, white bread
crumbs

For the red wine sauce
1½ cups beef stock (see page
17)
½ cup dry red wine
1 tbs. butter
2 tbs. flour
Salt
Pepper

To prepare the beef
Melt 2 tbs. of the butter in a small skillet, add onion and sauté 2 to 3 minutes. Add brandy, water, salt, pepper and Worcestershire sauce. Blend and pour into a mixing bowl; add remaining ingredients listed under meat, plus 1 tbs. of the remaining butter (which should be soft). Blend well, using hands dipped in cold water. Form into 4 patties.

Heat remaining butter in a heavy skillet; add beef patties. Brown on each side; then cook over medium heat until done to taste—rare or medium rare—but, please, not well done.

Serve with Red Wine Sauce.

Serves 4

To prepare the sauce
Combine stock and wine in a saucepan. Boil over high heat until reduced by half.

In a separate skillet, melt butter; stir in flour and cook over low heat until deep golden in color. Reheat and add reduced stock and wine. Cook, stirring, until sauce thickens. Season with salt and pepper. Pour over beef patties and serve at once.

GROUND BEEF PAPRIKA
WITH FLAT NOODLES

1 tbs. butter
1 large onion, peeled and
    minced
1 clove garlic, peeled and
    minced
¾ lb. lean ground beef
1 tbs. paprika
3 medium-size fresh tomatoes,
    chopped

½ cup beef stock (see page 17)
1 tsp. Worcestershire sauce
1 cup sour cream
Salt
1 lb. flat noodles cooked
    according to package
    directions

Melt the butter in a large deep skillet over low heat and add onion and garlic. Sauté until limp. Add beef and cook, stirring, until no longer pink. Stir in paprika, add tomatoes and stock. Partially cover and let simmer for 30 minutes, stirring occasionally. Stir in Worcestershire sauce and sour cream. Taste and add salt as desired.

Serve very hot over freshly cooked flat noodles.

Serves 6

MEAT BALLS
GREEK STYLE

1 small eggplant
1 lb. ground lean lamb
½ cup soft, fresh bread
    crumbs
1 egg, lightly beaten
2 tsp. cornstarch
1 tsp. seasoned salt
¼ tsp. pepper
3 tbs. oil

2 tbs. butter
1 small onion, peeled and
    chopped
2 tbs. flour
⅛ tsp. dry mustard
1½ cups chicken stock, heated
2 tbs. Madeira or dry sherry
    (optional)

Peel and finely chop the eggplant. Combine with lamb, bread crumbs, egg, cornstarch, salt, and pepper. Form into 24 small balls.

Heat the oil in a heavy skillet. In it brown the balls a few at a time on all sides, removing as browned. Set aside.

Pour oil from skillet and discard. Replace with butter; when melted, add onion and sauté until limp. Stir in flour; then add heated stock and stir until blended. Return meat balls to skillet. Cover and let simmer very gently for 25 to 30 minutes. Uncover, add Madeira or sherry and continue to cook a final 10 minutes.

Serve over just-cooked fluffy brown or white rice.

Serves 6 to 8

STUFFED GREEN PEPPERS

This stuffing is without the usual tomato sauce.

4 large, crisp, green peppers
4 tbs. butter
½ cup onion, finely minced
1 clove of garlic, finely minced
1 cup leftover pot roast, finely minced or braised ham (see recipes pages 19, 21) or any other leftover cooked meat
3 cups cooked rice

½ tsp. salt (or to taste)
¼ tsp. coarsely ground black pepper
¼ cup parsley, minced
2 tsp. red wine or apple cider vinegar
1 egg lightly beaten
3 tbs. fine, dry bread crumbs
1 cup chicken stock (see page 18)

Preheat oven to 375°F.

Cut peppers in half lengthwise, remove seeds, and cut away the thick inner white ribs. Drop them in a large pot of boiling water; let boil 8 to 10 minutes, then remove and immediately plunge them into cold water to stop their cooking.

To Prepare Filling

Melt 3 tbs. of the butter in a large pot; add the onion and garlic and sauté over low heat until limp. Remove pot from heat; add beef or ham, and rice; blend. Season with salt and pepper. Stir in parsley and vinegar, then egg. Mix thoroughly.

Fill peppers with mixture and arrange them side by side in a buttered shallow baking dish, just large enough to hold them. Sprinkle with bread crumbs and dot with slivers of the remaining butter. Pour the chicken stock into the pan and bake in preheated oven for 25 to 30 minutes or until peppers are tender and filling is firm.

Makes 8 stuffed pepper halves

MOUSSAKA

Tomato sauce

1 tbs. butter
½ cup onion, minced
½ lb. ground beef
1 1-lb. can stewed tomatoes
2 cups beef stock or water
1 6-oz. can tomato paste
½ tsp. mixed Italian herbs

2 eggplant (1 lb. each or a
   little over)
Salt
½ cup butter, melted

Cream sauce

2 tbs. butter
2 tbs. flour
½ tsp. salt
1½ cups milk
½ cup dry white wine
2 eggs
½ cup Parmesan cheese,
   grated
½ cup dry bread crumbs

To prepare tomato sauce

Melt the butter in a large deep skillet over low heat; add onions and sauté until limp. Stir in meat and cook, stirring until no longer pink. Add remaining ingredients and let simmer, stirring frequently until sauce is thick, about 45 minutes.

To prepare eggplant

Halve unpeeled eggplants lengthwise, slice crosswide in ½-inch thick pieces. Place in bottom of broiler pan, sprinkle lightly with salt and brush lightly with melted butter. Broil 4 inches from heat for 5 minutes. Turn and brush second side with butter and broil for another 5 minutes. Set aside.

To prepare cream sauce

Melt butter in a saucepan and stir in flour; when blended, slowly add milk, stirring. Add wine and stir until sauce thickens. Remove from heat. Add a little of the hot sauce to the beaten eggs, beating rapidly with a whisk. Then stir rapidly into the hot sauce. Return pan to heat and cook, stirring 2 to 3 minutes.

Preheat oven to 350°F.

To assemble casserole

In the bottom of a 2-quart, lightly greased, long, shallow baking dish, layer half of the eggplant, overlapping slightly. Sprinkle with 2 tbs. of grated cheese and all of bread crumbs. Pour tomato sauce over surface and sprinkle with another 2 tbs. of the grated cheese. Layer rest of eggplant slices, overlapping as before. Pour cream sauce over all and sprinkle top with remaining cheese. Bake 35 to 40 minutes or until top is golden brown and set.

Let stand 10 minutes at room temperature before serving. Cut into squares.

Serves 12

Notes

The original recipe called for 1½ lbs. meat, canned tomato sauce, 4 different spices and grated cheddar cheese. Inexpensive it was *not;* moreover, the final dish was heavy and over seasoned. This version is light but filling and tastes great at about half the price.

MEAT LOAF

1 tbs. butter
1 small onion, peeled and
    finely minced
1 clove garlic, finely minced
1 lb. chopped lean beef
    (Whatever you do, go to a
    reliable butcher for this;
    ask him to trim off the fat
    and grind it before your
    eyes—only this way will
    you get the fresh beef
    flavor that makes a little
    meat go a long way.)

¼ lb. salt pork chopped a
    very fine dice (free of
    rind)
1 cup milk
2 eggs, slightly beaten
1 tbs. prepared horseradish
2 cups soft bread crumbs
3 thin strips salt pork (free of
    rind)

Preheat oven to 300°F.—*no higher.*

Melt the butter in a small skillet over very low heat; in it sauté the onion and garlic until limp. Combine beef, pork cubes, milk, eggs, horseradish and bread crumbs in a large bowl; then add sautéed onions and garlic. Mix well to blend. Pour into lightly greased loaf pan and arrange pork slices evenly on top. Bake in preheated oven for 1 hour or until well brown and loaf shrinks from the side of the pan. The secret of meat loaf is the slow cooking; high heat will form a tasteless hard crust and the loaf will be dry and crumbly. Cool slightly before removing from the pan and slicing into serving portions.

Serves hot or cold.

Serves 6 to 8

PARTIES ON A BUDGET

If you love to entertain—who doesn't?—but you hate what a really great party does to your budget, then try a hamburger party. Yes, I know, even hamburger is expensive, but with a

lot of great tasting but inexpensive "go withs" you don't need
all that much meat, and I guarantee that your guests will have
a marvelous meal and a very good time. Mine certainly did,
for I've party tested each of the following menus on any
number of friends.

ALL-AMERICAN, STAR-SPANGLED, HAMBURGER PARTIES MENUS AND RECIPES

(asterisk indicates recipe to be found in this book)

TEXAS BURGER BARBECUE
(Big party-small house? Plan it for the great outdoors.)

HAMBURGERS
WITH
TEXAS BARBECUE SAUCE *
TEXAS TOMATO SALAD *
WESTERN BAKED BEANS *
BEER
SOUTHERN AMBROSIA *
"ANYTHING GOES" COOKIES *

Make aheads include Barbecue Sauce (page 58), Texas Tomato Salad (page 162), Baked Beans Texas Style (page 145),
Ambrosia (page 183) and cookies.

What's left to do? Start the fire about 3 hours before guests
are due to arrive. Prepare the raw hamburger patties. Put the
beer in a big bucket of ice (stick several can openers in with
them). Set the table, get ready for the party yourself (blue
jeans and western shirt are appropriate gear), then bring out
the food. Party's begun.

HAMBURGERS WITH TEXAS
BARBECUE SAUCE

3 lbs. hamburger meat   2 eggs, lightly beaten
1 cup soft bread crumbs   ¼ cup dry red wine

Combine ingredients in large mixing bowl and mix well. Shape into 12 patties. Refrigerate until 30 minutes before cooking. Broil over glowing coals until done to your taste. Brush with Barbecue Sauce while grilling (recipe follows).
Serves 12

BARBECUE SAUCE

1 tbs. brown sugar   1 tbs. vinegar
1 tbs. chili powder   1 cup tomato juice
2 tsp. dry mustard   2 tbs. tomato paste
1 tsp. salt
1 tsp. coarsely ground black
     pepper

Blend dry ingredients with vinegar in small sauce pan. Stir in remaining ingredients and beat with a whisk until well blended. Heat on barbecue grill to use for basting meat.

BRIDGE LUNCH FOR THE GIRLS

(asterisk indicates recipe to be found in book)

FRESH TOMATO-CUCUMBER SHRUB *
SERVED IN SHERBERT GLASSES
WITH SPRIGS OF FRESH MINT
DUTCHESS BURGERS *
DUTCHESS POTATOES *

CALIFORNIA DRY RED WINE
FRESH FRUIT COMPOTE
TO SPOON OVER
SPONGE CAKE WEDGES *
COFFEE

"Make aheads" include Tomato Shrub (page 149), fresh fruit compote, and Sponge Cake (page 187). What's left to do? About one hour before guests are due to arrive, set the table, open the wine, prepare hamburger patties, tomato slices and Dutchess Potatoes (keep hot), and coffee (again keep hot). Leave the Dutchess Burgers to prepare after guests arrive—it only takes about 10 minutes. Serve the first course and enjoy it with your guests; then pour them a first glass of wine to sip while you switch roles from hostess to cook and back again before they are ready for seconds to go with the main course.

DUTCHESS BURGERS

1 large ripe tomato
1 lb. lean ground beef
4 slices light rye bread

Butter
Dutchess Potatoes (recipe
follows)

Cut tomato into 4 thick slices (save end pieces for another use). Shape meat into 4 patties. Broil under high heat 5 minutes on each side.

Toast bread on one side only. Butter untoasted side. Place a meat pattie in center of each and top with tomato slice. Surround with Dutchess Potatoes, covering edges of bread completely. Place slivers of butter on tomato slices and potatoes. Place under medium broiler heat and broil until potatoes are flecked with brown.

Serves 4

DUTCHESS POTATOES

1 large potato
1 tbs. butter, room
    temperature
2 tbs. milk, room temperature

1 egg yolk, lightly beaten,
    room temperature
Salt

Boil potato in water to cover until done. Peel, and mash; while hot, beat in butter and milk, then egg yolk. Season with salt.

SWEDISH HAMBURGERS

1½ lbs. lean ground beef
1½ cups soft, white bread
    crumbs
2 tbs. onion, finely minced
2 tsp. salt
3 tbs. butter, room
    temperature

2 cups beef stock (see page 17)
1 tbs. flour
½ cup sour cream
Salt
Pepper
3 hamburger buns split and
    toasted

Preheat oven to 350°F.

Mix together beef, bread crumbs, onion, salt and 2 tbs. of the butter. Form into 12 patties.

Place patties in lightly greased shallow baking dish, about 3 inches under heat until lightly browned, turning once.

Pour stock into baking dish. Cover with light-fitting lid. Bake ½ hour.

Remove meat patties from pan with a slotted spatula. Keep warm. Reserve 1 cup of stock.

Melt remaining 1 tbs. butter in a saucepan. Stir in flour. When blended, slowly add the reserved 1 cup of stock and cook, stirring to a smooth thick sauce. Stir in sour cream, season with salt and pepper.

Place two meat patties on each half toasted bun. Spoon sauce over and serve at once.

Makes 6 hamburgers

CALIFORNIA CHEESEBURGERS

1½ lbs. lean ground beef
2 tsp. salt
1 tsp. Spice Parisienne
¼ tsp. coarsely ground black
    pepper
2 tbs. heavy cream
2 tbs. butter
¼ lb. crumbled blue cheese
3 hamburger buns
1 head Boston lettuce,
    shredded

1 small tomato, seeded and
    chopped
1 small avocado, peeled,
    seeded and chopped
    (optional)
1 medium size purple onion,
    peeled and sliced as thinly
    as possible
6 tbs. vinaigrette dressing

Mix together beef, salt, Spice Parisienne, pepper, and cream. Form into 6 patties. Preheat broiler for 10 minutes. Place beef patties on lightly greased broiler rack, about 3 inches below heat. Broil 5 to 6 minutes on each side.

Cream butter with cheese and spread mixture on split hamburger rolls. Place under broiler heat until toasted.

Place a meat pattie on each half bun.

Combine remaining ingredients and pile on top of each cheeseburger, dividing equally.

Serve at once.

Makes 6 cheeseburgers

FRIED SALT PORK SLICES
WITH CREAM GRAVY

Down here in North Carolina a favorite winter time supper dish is fried salt pork slices with cream gravy. It's usually served with fried apple slices and hot biscuits. No, it isn't exactly "no cal," but it's awfully good and you can have grapefruit salad tomorrow.

8 medium-thick slices salt pork
2 tbs. flour

1 cup milk, (or ½ cup milk
            and ½ cup chicken stock)
½ tsp. black pepper

In a large heavy skillet fry the pork slices over very low heat until crisp. This takes about 30 to 40 minutes, but don't rush it; the slices should be crisp all the way through. Remove from heat, drain on absorbent paper, place in a shallow baking dish and keep hot in a medium oven. Pour off all but about 2 tbs. of the accumulated fat in the skillet. Stir in flour and cook over very low heat for 3 to 4 minutes, stirring constantly. Slowly add the milk or milk and chicken stock and stir to blend well. Continue to cook, stirring, until gravy is thick and smooth. Stir in pepper. Pour over salt pork slices and serve very hot.
    Serves 4

BEEF AND POTATO BURGERS
WITH CHILI SAUCE

¼ lb. salt pork cubes, rind
    removed and finely
    chopped
2 large California white
    potatoes
1 small onion
1 lb. lean ground beef

1 tsp. Worcestershire sauce
1 tsp. salt
¼ tsp. coarsely ground black
    pepper
3 hamburger buns split and
    toasted
Chili Sauce (recipe follows)

Rinse loose salt from salt pork cubes under cold water. Blot thoroughly dry.
    Place in a large heavy skillet over low medium heat until fat has been rendered and cubes are crisp. Remove crisp cubes. Drain. (Store in a small refrigerator dish, add to a tossed green salad, add to baked beans or use as desired.)
    Set skillet with rendered fat aside (off heat) until ready to use.

Peel and grate potato and onion on coarse side of grater. Place in a mixing bowl; add meat and seasonings. Mix well and form into 6 patties.

Reheat fat in skillet. Fry patties in hot fat, turning frequently for 15 to 20 minutes.

Place 1 pattie on each half bun. Spoon Chili Sauce over surface and serve at once.

Serves 6

CHILI SAUCE

1 cup tomato sauce or tomato
    ketchup
½ cup sugar

2 tbs. vinegar
½ tsp. dry mustard

Combine ingredients in saucepan and cook, stirring, over low heat until sugar is dissolved and mixture heated.

BIFF A LA LINDSTROM

2 medium size California
    white potatoes
1 lb. lean ground beef
2 egg yolks
½ cup sour cream
½ tsp. dry mustard
½ tsp. salt
¼ tsp. pepper

¼ cup cooked beets, finely
    diced (thoroughly drained
    if using canned beets)
1 tsp. Worcestershire sauce
2 tbs. butter
Sour Cream Horseradish
    Sauce (recipe follows)

Boil potatoes in water to cover until done. Cool, then peel and chop finely.

Place meat in a mixing bowl and, using a pestle or an old-fashioned potato masher, make as smooth a paste as possible. Mix the egg yolks with the sour cream and gradually add to the meat, continuing to pound while mixing. Mix in mustard, salt and pepper. Add finely diced potatoes and beets, and Worcestershire sauce. Blend well and form into small cakes about ½-inch thick.

Melt butter in a heavy skillet over high heat. Add meat cakes and fry quickly, turning once to brown on both sides.

Serves 6

SOUR CREAM HORSERADISH SAUCE

¾ cup sour cream   ¼ cup (bottled) horseradish

Bring to room temperature and blend well.

CREOLE KIDNEY STEW

4 veal kidneys   1 1-lb. can tomatoes
¼ lb. salt pork cut into cubes   1 cup beef stock or water
1 large, mild purple onion   ¼ cup dry red wine
1 medium-size green pepper   Flour
3 celery stalks   Salt
1 tbs. flour   Pepper

Wash the kidneys, cut in half and remove core. Soak in cold water for 1 hour.

Prepare sauce while kidneys soak.

Put the salt pork cubes in a heavy skillet over low heat until fat is rendered and cubes are crisp. Remove cubes and set aside. Remove about half the rendered fat and set aside.

Sauté the onion, green pepper and celery in the remaining fat until limp. Stir in the flour, then add the tomatoes, stock (or water) and wine. Bring to a boil, then lower heat and let simmer for about 30 minutes.

Drain the kidneys, blot dry and cut them into small pieces. Dredge lightly in flour.

Heat remaining rendered pork fat in a small fry pan; brown the kidneys in it. Add them to the sauce and let simmer for a final 10 minutes.

Serve the stew over cooked brown or white rice.

Serves 6 to 8

SAUTÉED KIDNEYS ITALIAN STYLE
WITH PEAS AND ONIONS

6 veal kidneys	*¼ tsp. mixed Italian herbs*
2 tbs. butter	*2 cups green peas, cooked*
2 tbs. vermouth	*6 very small white onions,*
2 cups tomato sauce	*boiled*

Wash the kidneys and soak in cold water for 1 hour. Drain, and discard the core. Cut into small pieces.

Melt the butter in a small fry pan; sauté the kidneys in it for 1 minute. Stir in the vermouth and cook another minute. Add tomato sauce, herbs, peas and onions. Cook, stirring for 5 to 10 minutes and serve at once with hot, freshly cooked rice.

Serves 6

DEVILED KIDNEYS

4 veal kidneys	*1 tsp. lemon juice*
Flour	*1 tsp. Worcestershire sauce*
2 tbs. butter	*4 thick slices Italian bread,*
1 tsp. dry mustard	*heated*
1 cup beef stock (see page 17)	

Wash the kidneys, cut in half, remove fat and cores. Soak in cold water for 1 hour. Drain, pat dry and cut into slices. Dredge lightly in flour.

Melt the butter in a skillet; add kidneys and sauté for 1 minute. Stir in the mustard, add remaining ingredients and cook over medium heat, stirring almost constantly for 2 minutes. Spoon kidneys and sauce over heated bread and serve at once.

Twice as delicious as hamburgers. Less expensive too.

Serves 4

IRISH STEW

2 lbs. of lamb neck or shoulder
    (or any combination
      special)
2 lbs. onions
3 lbs. potatoes

3 tsp. salt
1 tsp. pepper
3 to 4 cups fat-free chicken
    stock (see page 18)
Chopped parsley

Cut the meat into chunks, including the bone, cut off and discard excess fat.

Peel the onions and cut into ¼-inch slices. Pare the potatoes and cut into ¼-inch slices.

Arrange half of the potatoes and onions in a 2-quart flame-proof casserole. Sprinkle with salt and pepper. Add the meat, sprinkle with salt and pepper; then add remaining onions and top with remaining potatoes, and again sprinkle with salt and pepper.

Pour in sufficient chicken stock to almost but not quite cover last layer of potatoes.

Bring to a boil. Cover, lower heat and let simmer until meat and vegetables are tender, about 1½ hours.

Sprinkle with parsley just before serving.

Serves 6

Notes

The secret of great flavor in an Irish stew is in the liquid in which it is cooked. Well-seasoned, homemade chicken stock will produce a superb dish. If you don't have it on hand, use canned chicken broth and cut down on the salt—it's salty—and add to the salt and pepper about 1 tsp. Spice Parisienne.

PORK, APPLES AND SAUERKRAUT

1 lb. boneless lean pork cut
    into 1-inch cubes
3 cloves garlic, peeled and cut
    in half lengthwise
1 tsp. salt
2 cups water
2 tbs. pork fat diced (or butter)
1 1-lb. 13 oz. can sauerkraut,
    drained

2 medium-size tart apples,
    peeled, cored, seeded and
    chopped
1 medium-size onion, peeled
    and chopped
1 tbs. prepared mustard
1 tbs. prepared horseradish
1/8 tsp. coarsely ground black
    pepper

Ask for the pork fat used in this recipe when you buy the meat. A friendly butcher will give it to you. If he's not—friendly that is—he can only charge pennies for it.

Place the meat, garlic, salt and water in a skillet. Bring to a boil; then lower heat, partially cover pot and let simmer for about 1½ hours. Add additional water as needed and keep meat covered. Drain meat cubes and blot dry. Discard garlic.

Place diced pork fat cubes in 2-quart casserole (one that can be used on top of the stove). Fry, stirring frequently, until fat is rendered. Remove and discard the cubes. Add the pork and cook, stirring until lightly browned. Pour and discard cooking fat.

Combine remaining ingredients and add to casserole. Fork stir so that meat is evenly distributed.

Cover and place in a preheated 350°F. oven. Bake 30 minutes. Uncover and bake 30 minutes longer.

Serve from the casserole.

Serves 4 to 6

BEANS WITH HAM AND VEGETABLES
BASQUE STYLE

1 cup dried white beans
2 tbs. butter
1 large onion, peeled and
    chopped
1 clove garlic, peeled and
    minced
1 lb. smoked ham butt or
    shoulder
¼ tsp. Spice Parisienne (or if
    available 1 sprig fresh
    marjoram and 1 sprig
    fresh rosemary)
1 small cauliflower, trimmed
    and broken into
    flowerettes

1½ cups fresh green beans (or
    1 10-oz. package frozen
    whole green beans,
    sufficiently thawed to
    separate beans)
1 small cabbage, washed and
    quartered
Salt
Pepper
Horseradish sauce (see
    page 64)

Cover beans with warm water and soak for 2 hours. Drain.

In a large, heavy stew pot melt the butter. Add the onion and garlic and sauté until limp. Place the ham in the pot, and add the beans and cover with fresh water by about 2 inches. Add Spice Parisienne or fresh herbs. Bring to a boil; then lower heat, partially cover pot and let simmer for 2 hours. Add cauliflower and beans, pushing them down into the pot. Simmer partially covered for about 30 minutes or until vegetables are tender. Place cabbage wedges on top of mixture and cook covered a final 15 minutes. Season with salt and pepper to taste.

Remove and slice meat. Place on a large platter and surround with vegetables. Pass Horseradish sauce separately.

Serves 6 to 8

CHOUCROUTE

3 lbs. sauerkraut, fresh or
    canned
½ lb. salt pork
3 cups chicken stock (see page
    18)
½ tsp. dry mustard
1 cup dry white wine or dry
    vermouth

6 small onions, peeled and
    quartered
3 large carrots, scraped and
    cut into 2-inch pieces
8 knockwursts

Preheat oven to 325°F.

Place sauerkraut in a pan of cold water. Rinse well and squeeze dry. Pull it apart to loosen any lumps.

Cut the salt pork into thin slices. Place in a small pan and cover with water. Bring to a boil and let boil five minutes. Drain. Pat dry.

Cover the bottom of a heavy, large oven-proof pot with the pork slices, and add the sauerkraut. Mix a little of the stock with the mustard to make a paste. Stir this into the stock and pour over the sauerkraut. Add the wine and push the onions and carrots down into the sauerkraut. Bring the liquid to a boil on top of the stove; then cover, place in the preheated oven and bake for 2½ hours. Arrange the knockwursts over the sauerkraut. Cover and bake a final half hour.

Serves 8

Notes

If you have it on hand, add about ¼ cup good quality gin, when adding the wine.

Also, if you like, add a peeled and minced clove of garlic, and/or a peeled, cored and finely minced tart apple.

PUERCO CON FRIJOLES
(Cuban Pork with Beans)

3 cups dried black beans
3 tsp. salt
¼ tsp. pepper
1 large onion, peeled and
    chopped
2 cloves garlic, peeled and
    minced
1 lb. boneless pork cut into
    1-inch cubes

Water, as needed
2 tsp. chili powder
3 to 4 cups cooked white rice
½ cup chopped onion
1 cup cheddar cheese,
    shredded

Place beans in a large pot and cover with water. Bring to a full boil. Remove from heat and let stand for 2 hours. Again bring to a boil, lower heat and let simmer for 1 hour. Add salt, pepper, onion and garlic and let simmer while browning meat.

Place pork cubes in a broiling pan in a preheated 375°F. oven until browned. Turn them several times to insure even browning. Drain and add to beans. Stir in chili powder and continue to simmer until meat and beans are tender.

Serve over hot just-cooked white or brown rice. Sprinkle chopped onions and grated cheese over each serving.

Serves 6

PORK CHOW MEIN

This is authentic chow mein. There is no need to buy expensive so-called Chinese vegetables—the Chinese don't, I assure you.

*1 lb. boneless pork cut into
    small dice
2 tbs. vegetable oil
2 large onions, peeled and
    diced
3 to 4 celery stalks, cut
    diagonally into thin slices
1 medium-size white turnip,
    peeled and sliced, slices
    cut into matchlike slices*

*2 tbs. water
1 cup shredded cabbage
¼ cup soy sauce
3 tbs. cornstarch
2 cups chicken or beef stock
    (see pages 17 and 18)
3 cups cooked white rice*

Stir-fry the pork in the oil in a heavy skillet over low heat until the meat is no longer pink. Add the onions, celery and turnips, and stir-fry until vegetables are coated with oil; add water, then cover and steam for 5 minutes. Add cabbage. Stir-fry for 1 minute, then cover and steam 5 additional minutes.

Combine soy sauce and cornstarch and stir until smooth. Stir in stock. Add mixture to pork and vegetables and cook, stirring, for 3 to 4 minutes.

Serve over just-cooked hot white rice.

Serves 6

STIR-FRIED PORK WITH FRESH GREEN PEPPERS

*3 large green peppers
4 1½-inch thick shoulder pork
    chops
1½ cups chicken stock (see
    page 18)*

*1 tsp. sugar
2 tbs. soy sauce
½ tsp. cornstarch
3 tbs. dry sherry
Cooked white rice*

Wash peppers, cut in half, remove seeds and white part. Cut each half into 1-inch squares. Place in saucepan and cover with water. Bring to a full boil, lower heat and let simmer for 10 minutes. Drain. Set aside.

Remove bone and fat from chops and discard bone. Cut meat into thin strips and set aside. Cut fat into small dice and place in a large, deep, heavy skillet over low heat. Cook, stirring occasionally, until rendered and skillet is covered with a film of fat. Remove and discard the dry pork fat dice.

Turn heat to high, add meat strips and stir-fry until they color and are flecked with brown. Add stock, reduce heat and partially cover skillet. Let simmer 30 minutes. Add green pepper. Stir to blend and let simmer, partially covered, for about 5 minutes or until peppers are cooked but still crisp. Add sugar and soy sauce.

Mix cornstarch into sherry and slowly pour into skillet. Stir until sauce thickens and a clear glaze coats meat and peppers.

Serve immediately over just-cooked hot and fluffy white rice.

Serves 4 to 6

CHINESE FRIED RICE WITH PORK OR HAM

*1 cup chopped, cooked pork or
    ham*
4 to 6 green onions
*1 small green pepper, seeded
    and cut into very thin
    slivers*

2 tbs. vegetable oil
*3 cups day-old cold cooked
    rice*
2 tbs. soy sauce
2 eggs, well beaten
Soy sauce, as desired

In a heavy skillet stir-fry meat, onion and pepper in oil for 2 to 3 minutes. Add rice and pork and stir until heated.

Add soy sauce. Pour in eggs and continue to cook, stirring gently with fork until mixture is dry; add additional soy sauce to taste. Serve very hot.

Serves 6

PIEDS DE PORC GRILLÉS

6 pigs' feet
2 carrots, scraped and cut in
    several pieces
2 onions, peeled and quartered
12 pepper corns
3 cloves
2 celery stalks

3 tbs. cider vinegar
1 tbs. dry mustard mixed with
    1 tbs. water to make a
    paste
½ cup fine, dry bread crumbs
½ cup melted butter

Wash the pigs' feet thoroughly and place in a deep, heavy 4- to 6-quart pot. Add carrots, onions, pepper corns, cloves, celery and vinegar. Add sufficient water to come to about 2 inches of rim of pot. Place over very low heat, partially cover pot and let simmer for 4 hours; or place all in crockpot, cover and cook on low for 8 to 10 hours.

Drain the pigs' feet and wipe them dry. Brush evenly with mustard paste and roll in bread crumbs. Place in a shallow, buttered baking dish (or in bottom of roasting pan), sprinkle with melted butter. Place under high broiler heat until crumbs are lightly browned.

Serves 6

Notes

It's fine meal served with roasted potatoes and crisp cold slaw.

ROASTED POTATOES

6 medium size California
    white potatoes

Place potatoes in a large pot and cover with water. Let simmer until they can be pierced easily with a small sharp knife. Drain and cool slightly. Peel and cut in quarters. Place in a greased baking dish and bake until lightly browned.

SAUSAGE AND NOODLE CASSEROLE

½ lb. bulk country sausage
1 small green pepper, seeded,
    all white removed, and
    chopped
1 medium-size onion, peeled
    and chopped

3 or 4 celery stalks, chopped
2 cups stewed tomatoes
1 tbs. tomato paste
¼ tsp. mixed Italian herbs
½ tsp. salt
1 1-lb. package flat noodles

Put sausage, green pepper, onion and celery in a heavy skillet, cook, stirring often over low heat until vegetables are tender. Pour off and discard as much fat as possible. Add the tomatoes, tomato paste and season with herbs, salt and pepper. Blend and let simmer over low heat while cooking noodles according to package directions.

Drain noodles, place in a 2-quart casserole. Pour sausage mixture over surface and bake in a preheated 350°F. oven for 30 to 35 minutes.

Serves 4 to 6

SWEET AND SOUR CABBAGE
WITH FRANKFURTERS

1 medium head fresh green
    cabbage
1 tbs. butter
8 knockwursts or frankfurters
1 tbs. red wine vinegar or
    apple cider vinegar

¼ cup water
½ tsp. salt
1 tbs. sugar

Remove and discard tough outer leaves from cabbage, cut into four wedges. Remove and discard core. Place in a large bowl, sprinkle generously with salt and cover with cold water. Let stand a few minutes. Drain and rinse with clear water.

Melt the butter in a large heavy skillet—one with a tight-fitting lid. Add the cabbage wedges and top with the knock-wurst. Combine remaining ingredients and pour into skillet. Cover tightly and let steam-cook for 15 minutes or until cabbage has lost its raw taste but is still quite crisp and knock-wurst is heated.

Add steamed new or baked potatoes and dinner is served. Serves 4

ALSATIAN BRAISED CABBAGE
WITH FRANKFURTERS

1 large, firm, very fresh green cabbage	1 tbs. sugar
	1 tsp. salt
Salt	⅓ cup water
1 large tart apple	3 tbs. green pepper jelly (see
1 small onion	page 174)
2 tbs. butter	8 top-quality frankfurters
¼ cup apple cider vinegar	

Strip the outer leaves from the cabbage and cut it into quarters from top to bottom, and cut away the core. Place the quarters in a large bowl of cold, heavily salted water and let stand about 15 minutes. Drain and rinse under cold water. Lay each quarter flat side down on a chopping board and slice it crosswise as finely as possible.

Peel, core and finely chop the apple; peel and mince onion. Combine cabbage, apple, and onion in a large 4- to 5-quart heavy casserole equipped with a tight-fitting cover.

Preheat oven to 375°F.

Combine the butter, vinegar, sugar, salt and water in a small saucepan. Bring to a boil over high heat and stir until butter has melted. Pour over cabbage mixture, and toss gently with two forks to blend.

Cover the casserole and bake in preheated oven for 2 hours. (Check occasionally and add a little hot water if necessary). Cabbage should be faintly moist but not swimming in liquid during the entire period.

Uncover and stir in jelly. Place frankfurters over cabbage. Cover tightly again and bake a final 15 to 20 minutes or until frankfurters are heated.

Serves 6 to 8

Notes

If you have leftover baked ham on hand use it instead of the frankfurters, or eliminate meat from this dish and serve with braised pork chops, broiled or pan braised, or browned little link sausage.

If you don't have or want to make the pepper jelly, you can eliminate this ingredient and for extra flavor use light brown instead of white sugar in the cooking liquid.

SAUSAGE-STUFFED SUMMER SQUASH

This makes for a hearty main dish when the need is for something substantial in every direction except price. I like to add broiled tomatoes, made special by topping with a bit of green pepper jelly (see page 174) and end the meal with something hearty like deep-dish blueberry or peach pie served with just a bit of sour cream.

6 large yellow squash
1 tbs. butter
1 onion, finely minced
½ lb. bulk sausage—country sausage if available because its more flavorful and less expensive
½ cup water

1 cup fine, dry bread crumbs
½ tsp. salt
½ tsp. coarsely ground black pepper
1 tbs. Parmesan cheese, grated
1 tbs. butter
¼ cup water

Cut the squash in half lengthwise; with a teaspoon carefully scoop out the pulp, taking care not to break the outer shell. Place pulp in a mixing bowl and chop fine. Melt the butter in a heavy skillet, add the minced onion and sauté over low heat until limp. Add sausage and water and cook over low heat until sausage is no longer pink; break up meat with a fork as it cooks. Add onion and meat mixture, salt, pepper and Parmesan cheese to chopped squash. Blend well. Pack into hollowed-out squash shells, mounding slightly. Dot with slivers of butter. Place in shallow oven casserole, pour in water, cover and bake in 300°F. oven for 1 hour. Uncover during last 15 minutes of baking to brown lightly.

Serves 6

OLD-FASHIONED
CORN AND HAM PUDDING

This is a supper dish that most men enjoy.

2 tbs. butter
¼ cup green pepper, minced
¼ cup onion, minced
1 tbs. flour
1 1-lb. can cream-style corn
¼ cup lean, leftover braised
    ham, minced

3 eggs, separated
2 to 3 dashes hot pepper sauce
    (see page 179)
Dash Worcestershire sauce
½ tsp. salt
⅛ tsp. pepper

Preheat oven to 350°F.

Butter a 1½ quart shallow baking dish.

Melt the butter in a large, heavy skillet; add green pepper and onion. Cook, stirring until vegetables are soft. Stir in flour and add corn and ham. Blend. Remove from heat to a large bowl. Cool to lukewarm.

Add egg yolks, hot pepper sauce, Worcestershire, salt and pepper.

Beat egg whites until stiff. Fold into corn mixture. Pour into prepared baking dish.

Bake in preheated oven until firm, about 25 minutes.

Serves 4 to 6

LOUISIANA HAM AND VEGETABLE
JAMBALAYA

1 cup baked leftover ham,
   diced (cut cubes with a bit
   of fat)
2 large, fresh tomatoes,
   chopped
2 cups cooked, dried or fresh
   lima beans

1½ cups fresh corn
2 tbs. tomato ketchup
1 tsp. sugar
½ tsp. seasoned salt
¼ tsp. pepper
3 cups cooked brown or white
   rice

In a large, deep, heavy skillet sauté ham cubes over low heat until fat is crisp and cubes flecked with brown. Add the chopped tomatoes and cook, chopping them still further with the tip of a spatula until reduced to a chunky pulp.

Add lima beans and corn to the skillet along with the seasonings. Cook, stirring, until corn is tender and mixture is heated.

Serve over just-cooked rice.

Serves 6 to 8

SUNDAY BREAKFAST CORNED BEEF HASH
WITH POACHED EGGS AND AVOCADO

This dish is a smash hit each time it's served. Just everybody goes for it. Here's one instance where a canned prepared food is much less expensive than making your own. Nutrition is stepped up by the eggs and avocado. However, if avocados are not local or on special, you can substitute bananas—they are nearly always at bargain price—or just about any other fruit that's in season and economical.

3 tbs. butter, or use part
     rendered salt pork fat
1 clove garlic, minced
½ cup onion, chopped,
½ cup green pepper, chopped
     (or use just onion if green
     peppers are overpriced)
2 1-lb. cans top-quality corned
     beef hash (don't skimp
     here—the better brands
     are worth the slight
     difference in price)

Salt
Pepper
Worcestershire sauce
Hot pepper sauce (see page
     179)
6 eggs
1 medium-size avocado, (or 3
     medium-size bananas)

Preheat oven to 375°F.

Melt the butter in a large, heavy skillet—one with an oven-proof handle. Add the garlic, onion and green pepper (or what have you) and sauté until vegetables are limp. Add the hash and break up with a spatula. Cook, stirring until heated. Season to taste—I'm generous with seasoning for this dish—with salt, pepper, Worcestershire sauce and hot pepper sauce.

(You can prepare the hash ahead if you like. Keep at room temperature and add the egg when ready to proceed.)

With the back of a tablespoon make 6 indentions in the hash. Break one egg into each.

Cut avocado in half lengthwise and remove seed. Peel and cut into 6 wedges (or peel, slice bananas lengthwise and cut each half into 2 pieces). Arrange around edge of skillet. Cover and bake until egg whites are firm.

Serve from the dish.

Serves 6

TEXAS SAUSAGE

½ lb. bulk country sausage
4 cups water
1 tsp. salt

1 cup grits
½ cup cornmeal
Freshly ground black pepper

Cook sausage over low heat in a heavy skillet until no longer pink. Pour off all fat.

Bring the water to a boil in a large pot. Add salt and grits and stir for 3 to 3½ minutes. Add cornmeal and season with pepper. Mix thoroughly and cook, stirring, until thickened. Stir in sausage. Pour into a loaf pan. Refrigerate overnight.

When ready to serve cut into slices about ¾-inch thick and broil, turning once until crisp and browned.

Serves 8 or more

BREAKFAST HAM CAKES
SOUTHERN STYLE

2 cups water, or 1 cup milk   *¼ tsp. salt*
    and 1 cup water, or use   *⅓ cup grits*
    reconstituted dry skim milk   *1 4-oz. can deviled ham spread*

Bring water to a full boil. Add salt and grits, stirring as added. Reduce heat to simmering point and cook, stirring frequently until grits are smooth but still liquid. Add ham spread and stir until blended and mixture is thick. Pour into a buttered, shallow baking dish. Cool. Then cover and refrigerate until cold and firm.

Cut into ½-inch thick slices; place slices on, sides not touching, a greased baking sheet. Place about 3 inches under medium broiler heat and cook until flecked with brown. Using a spatula, turn slices and broil second side.

Serve very hot with poached or baked eggs; or serve with maple or cane syrup.

Serves 6

chapter four

All Manner of Chicken

CHICKEN—THE VERSATILE BIRD

Isn't it nice that chicken is not just cheap but liked by just about everybody? I have never heard anyone say "I hate chicken." Though there are no doubt thousands who hate lamb or fish, or they hate something or other, but chicken—no—to a man, Americans love it. And that's certainly handy for the thrifty cook, for with a little imagination and less work, chicken can be the star attraction for many a memorable meal. I've tried to include chicken recipes here that are a little off the beaten track since I'm sure you already have your own collection of sautéed, broiled, fried and baked chicken recipes. Here are a few of the ways I've served chicken successfully. I hope you will like them.

SUMMER PORCH PARTY
(CAN DOUBLE AS A COCKTAIL BUFFET IF DESIRED)

(asterisk indicates recipe to be found in this book)

MINIATURE BARBECUED CHICKEN ''LEGS'' *

MACARONI SALAD *

WHOLE CHERRY TOMATOES

UNPEELED CUCUMBER FINGERS

COLD BEER

OR COCKTAILS

(depending on the occasion)

DESSERT RICE RING

FOR FRESH FRUIT WITH

PEACH PUREE *

CHICKEN ITALIAN STYLE

CUCUMBERS MARINATED

IN VINAIGRETTE DRESSING *

DRY RED WINE

SPONGE CAKE WITH

FRESH BERRIES AND SOUR CREAM *

DEVILED CHICKEN *

ZUCCHINI, TOMATO AND CORN CASSEROLE *

CHILLED DRY WHITE WINE

TAPIOCA CUSTARD * WITH ANY

SUMMER FRUIT

WINTER

SPANISH CHICKEN

WITH GREEN PEPPER STRIPS *

RICE

CHILLED DRY WHITE WINE

INDIAN PUDDING *

SAUTÉED CHICKEN LIVERS *
WITH
RICE AND HOMEMADE CHUTNEY *
DRY WHITE WINE
OR COLD BEER
COLD (CANNED) SLICED BEETS WITH
VINAIGRETTE DRESSING *
BANANAS FLAMBÉ *
COFFEE

ROAST TURKEY OR CHICKEN
WITH DRESSING
(See Roast Turkey recipe page 22. Cut
dressing recipe in half for chicken and roast
chicken 10 minutes to the pound.)

DRY WHITE WINE
MASHED TURNIPS *
OLD-FASHIONED RICE PUDDING
WITH ORANGE-PEEL SAUCE *

HOW TO USE ONE CHICKEN
FOR TWO MAIN-COURSE DISHES AND
A GREAT SOUP

CHICKEN ITALIAN STYLE
ORIENTAL STIR-FRY CHICKEN BREASTS
POTAGE DE LÉGUMES DAVENPORT

Select a plump 3½- to 4-lb. fresh chicken.

Have the butcher remove the breast, skin and bone it and cut it in two pieces. Have the remaining chicken cut into serving pieces. Make sure he gives you the bones from the chicken breast plus the neck, gizzard and liver.

CHICKEN ITALIAN STYLE

Chicken pieces from a 3½- to
    4-lb. chicken, minus
    chicken breast, neck,
    gizzard and liver
1 tb. butter
1 clove garlic, peeled and
    minced
¾ cup dry red wine
1 1-lb. can tomatoes
1 medium-size fresh tomato,
    chopped

½ tsp. mixed Italian herbs
1 tbs. parsley stems, minced
¼ tsp. salt
Coarsely ground black pepper
2 to 3 dashes hot pepper sauce
    (see page 179)
1 lb. flat noodles or thin
    spaghetti

Preheat oven to 375°F.

Put chicken pieces in a large, heavy pot or casserole that can be used both in the oven and on top of the stove. Place in preheated oven a total of about 30 minutes. Turn each piece with a long-handled fork after 10 minutes. Then bake a final 10 minutes or until each piece is lightly browned.

Transfer to top of stove. Remove chicken pieces and set aside. Pour off and discard all but a thin film of the rendered fat. Add the butter and garlic and cook, stirring over moderate heat for about 1 minute. Add ¼ cup of the wine and let boil until reduced by about half. Return chicken pieces to the pot and add all remaining ingredients except noodles. Partially cover and let simmer over very low heat for about 45 minutes or until chicken is tender.

Cook noodles (or spaghetti) according to package directions for al dente—tender but still just slightly firm. Drain. Place on a warm platter or deep serving plates. Spoon chicken and sauce on top and serve at once.

Serves 6

ORIENTAL STIR-FRY CHICKEN BREASTS

1 *large chicken breast,*
    skinned, boned and cut in
    half
1 *large carrot*
1 *small cucumber*
4 *celery stalks*
1 *medium-size onion*
¼ *lb. tender, young spinach*
    leaves

2 *tbs. vegetable oil*
½ *cup chicken stock (see page*
    18)
2 *tbs. dry sherry*
2 *tsp. cornstarch mixed with 1*
    tbs. water
2 *tbs. soy sauce*
2 *cups just-cooked, hot white*
    or brown rice

First prepare chicken breast and all vegetables.

Cut chicken breast into bite-size cubes.

Scrape carrot, cut diagonally into the thinest possible oval slices. Drop slices into a small pan of boiling water. Boil 5 minutes. Drain.

Peel and cut cucumber in half, scrape out and discard seed. Cut each half into ¼-inch slices.

Slice celery diagonally.

Peel and chop onion.

Wash spinach thoroughly, remove and discard tough stems. Cut into thin shreds.

Heat oil in a heavy skillet, add onion and stir-fry 1 minute. Add carrot, celery and cucumber. Stir-fry 1 minute. Cover and let steam for 2 or 3 minutes.

Stir in chicken and cook, stirring until meat has turned white. Add stock and sherry. Bring to a boil. Reduce heat, cover and steam 2 to 3 minutes. Stir in cornstarch and water mixture. Add spinach. Stir-fry for 2 minutes. Stir in soy sauce. Turn out over just-cooked hot rice.

Serves 4

POTAGE DE LÉGUMES DAVENPORT

Stock

Bones from both chicken
    dishes
Chicken neck, giblet and liver
6 cups water
1 carrot, scraped and cut in
    several pieces
1 onion, peeled and cut in
    quarters

1 small clove garlic, peeled
¼ tsp. salt
Plus, if on hand
    A few chopped mushroom
    stems
    Several leafy celery tops
    A few chopped parsley
    stems

Place chicken bones, neck, giblet and liver in a large, heavy pot and add water. Bring to a boil and skim surface until clear. Add remaining ingredients, lower heat and let simmer for about 2 hours. (Remove liver after first 15 minutes and set aside.) Remove gizzard and set aside. Strain stock. Chop and add liver and gizzard. Refrigerate, covered, several hours, or until all fat has risen to surface and congealed. Remove and discard fat.

Soup

1 small onion, peeled and
    minced
1 small clove garlic, peeled
    and minced
1 tbs. butter
Stock from above
1 large potato, peeled and
    chopped
1 medium-size tomato, peeled
    and chopped

1 small Hubbbard (acorn)
    squash, peeled, seeded
    and chopped
½ cup vermicelli
1 cup (packed down) spinach
    leaves, shredded
Salt
Pepper
1 tbs. Parmesan cheese, grated

In a soup pot sauté the onion and garlic in the butter over low heat until soft. Add the stock, potato, tomato and squash. Simmer over low heat for about 45 minutes or until squash and potato are very tender. Add the vermicelli and continue to cook for about 10 minutes. Add spinach and cook a final 5 minutes. Season to taste with salt and pepper. Stir in cheese and serve steamy hot in deep bowls.

Serves 4

SPANISH CHICKEN
WITH GREEN PEPPER STRIPS

1 3- to 3½-lb chicken cut into
    8 serving pieces
1 clove garlic, peeled and
    finely minced
1 large onion cut lengthwise in
    half, then into ¼-inch
    wide strips
2 large green peppers and 1
    small sweet red pepper,
    all seeded, white part
    removed and cut
    lengthwise into ¼-inch
    wide strips

12 to 18 very thin 1-inch
    strips of lean baked or
    braised ham
4 cups stewed (fresh or
    canned) tomatoes
Salt
Pepper
2 to 3 drops hot pepper sauce
    (see page 179)
3 to 4 cups just-cooked, fluffy,
    dry white or brown rice

Preheat oven to 350°F.

Place chicken pieces, not touching, in a single layer in the bottom of a large, heavy skillet with heat-proof handle. Bake in preheated oven for about 30 minutes, or until each piece of chicken is lightly browned and the bottom of the skillet is coated with rendered fat.

Remove skillet from oven. Remove chicken and set aside.

Add garlic, onion, green and red peppers and ham to fat in skillet. Cook on top of the stove, stirring frequently, for 8 to 10 minutes. Return the chicken pieces to the skillet and add the tomatoes. Season lightly with salt, pepper and hot pepper sauce. Cover and let simmer until chicken is very tender, about 30 minutes. Serve over rice.

Serves 6

OVEN-BAKED CHICKEN
WITH ITALIAN SAUCE

1 2½- to 3-lb. chicken cut into serving pieces	2 tbs. tomato paste
1 1-lb. can tomatoes	½ tsp. mixed Italian herbs
	¼ cup dry red wine (optional)

Place chicken pieces, not touching, in a single layer in a long, shallow baking dish in a 375°F. oven. Bake for 45 minutes, turning several times.

Take dish from oven, remove chicken pieces and pour off all rendered fat, but do not wash dish. Use a spatula to scrape up any browned bits of chicken that have clung to the bottom and sides of the dish.

Combine remaining ingredients and blend well.

Return chicken to dish and spoon sauce mixture over each piece. Return dish to the heated oven. Bake 15 to 20 minutes, basting chicken pieces several times as they bake. Serve over freshly cooked pasta.

Serves 4 to 6

OVEN-BAKED CHICKEN
WITH MUSHROOM SAUCE

1 2½- to 3-lb. chicken cut into serving pieces	¼ cup dry white wine or vermouth
2 tbs. butter	Salt
4 to 6 fresh mushroom caps	Pepper
1 tbs. flour	
1 cup chicken stock (see page 18)	

Place chicken pieces, not touching, in a single layer in a large skillet with heat-proof handle in a 375°F. oven. Bake for 1 hour, turning chicken pieces several times as they bake. Remove skillet from oven. Transfer chicken pieces to a heated platter and keep warm.

Pour rendered fat from skillet, add butter and place over low heat. When butter has melted, add chopped mushroom caps and sauté until tender. Sprinkle with flour and cook, stirring, 1 or 2 minutes. Slowly add wine and continue to cook until sauce is thick and smooth. Season to taste with salt and pepper. Pour over chicken pieces and serve at once.

Great over freshly cooked, hot, dry rice.

Serves 4 to 6

LEMON-BAKED CHICKEN

Chicken baked this way tastes so great it's hard to believe it's so simple to prepare.

6 chicken legs, 6 chicken thighs	Salt
	½ cup lemon juice

Place chicken pieces, not touching, in a long, shallow baking dish. Place in a preheated 375°F. oven and bake for 30 minutes, turning once. Sprinkle each piece lightly with salt. Pour half of the lemon juice over them. Bake 15 minutes. Turn again, sprinkle with salt and pour remaining lemon juice over each. Bake a final 15 minutes.

Serves 6

MINIATURE BARBECUED
CHICKEN "LEGS"

This really is budget minded but festive.

12 chicken wings	1 tbs. vinegar
Juice from 1 lemon	1 tsp. hot pepper sauce
1 cup tomato juice	½ tsp. salt
3 tbs. sugar	1 clove garlic, peeled and split
2 tbs. Worcestershire sauce	in half

Cut the double wing portion from the meaty "leg" section. (Save wing portions for the stock pot by freezing in a tightly closed container.) Combine all remaining ingredients in a large, nonmetal bowl and blend. Add chicken legs, basting to make sure they are evenly coated with marinade. Cover and refrigerate 8 to 10 hours or overnight.

Preheat oven to 400°F.

Drain chicken "legs" (reserve marinade; remove and discard garlic) and place on the rack of a broiler pan. Bake in preheated oven 20 to 25 minutes, turning frequently and basting with remaining marinade.

Serve hot or cold with potato salad and cold beer. Fresh fruit for dessert, naturally—maybe ice-cold watermelon.

Serves 4

MANDARIN CHICKEN

12 to 16 chicken wings
1 1-inch piece fresh ginger, or
    ½ tsp. ground ginger
6 to 8 large fresh mushrooms,
    trimmed and thinly sliced
4 to 6 scallions cut in 2-inch
    pieces
¼ cup dry sherry
¼ cup soy sauce

1½ cups chicken stock (see
    page 18)
½ tsp. salt
1 tsp. sugar
1 tbs. cornstarch mixed with 3
    tbs. water
Just-cooked, fluffy, dry white
    rice

Preheat oven to 350°F.

Place chicken wings in a long, shallow pan in preheated oven until well browned and skin is crisp; turn once or twice to brown evenly on all sides. Remove from oven. Remove chicken wings from pan and set aside.

Spoon about 2 tbs. of the rendered chicken fat into a large skillet. Place over medium heat; add ginger, mushrooms and scallions. Cook, stirring for 3 to 4 minutes. Remove and discard fresh ginger. Stir in sherry, soy sauce and chicken stock.

Season with salt and sugar. Bring to a boil and add chicken wings. Lower heat, cover and let simmer for about 15 minutes. Stir in cornstarch mixture, and cook, stirring until sauce thickens.

Serve over rice.

Serves 3 to 4

STIR-FRIED
CHINESE CHICKEN AND VEGETABLES

This is a very inexpensive dish if you buy whole chickens and have the butcher remove the skin and bone the breasts. The remaining chicken can be refrigerated or frozen for another meal.

2 whole chicken breasts,
    skinned and boned and
    cut into bite-size cubes
2 tbs. vegetable oil
4 carrots, scraped and cut
    diagonally into thinnest
    possible oval slices

½ cup chicken stock
1 cup green onions, sliced
¼ cup soy sauce
2 tbs. dry sherry
3 cups cold, cooked white rice
Fried Noodles (recipe follows)

In a large, heavy skillet over high heat stir-fry the chicken cubes in the oil until white. Add the carrot slices and stock. Cover and let steam for 5 minutes. Uncover and cook over high heat until liquid is reduced by about half. Add green onions. Cover and steam for 2 or 3 minutes. Stir in soy sauce and sherry. Blend. Stir in rice and cook until heated. Serve with fried noodles.

Serves 4 to 6

CHINESE FRIED NOODLES

½ lb. fine noodles
2 tbs. vegetable oil

1 tsp. salt

Cook noodles as directed on package. Drain and chill.

Heat the oil in a heavy skillet. Add the noodles and salt, and stir-fry for 4 to 5 minutes. Drain.

DEVILED CHICKEN

12 chicken legs
4 tbs. butter, room
    temperature
½ tsp. dry mustard

½ tsp. Worcestershire sauce
1 cup fine, soft bread crumbs
    (homemade in blender
    from firm white bread)

Place chicken legs, not touching, in a single layer in a long, shallow baking dish. Place in a preheated 375°F. oven and bake for 30 minutes, turning occasionally.

While chicken bakes, whip butter until light. Add mustard and Worcestershire sauce and beat until blended.

Remove chicken from baking dish and set aside. Pour off and discard rendered fat from pan, but do not wash pan. Roll each chicken leg first in butter mixture then in bread crumbs and return them to the baking dish.

Bake 10 to 15 minutes. If desired, place briefly under broiler heat for a few minutes to brown.

Serves 6

CHICKEN CURRY

The best and most delicious curry starts with homemade stock. Stock again? Of course, it's the easy and inexpensive way. Poach the chicken, in water, plus seasoning vegetables; when the meat is sufficiently tender remove it from the bone. Put the bones back in the pot, add a bit of dry vermouth and simmer for about 1 hour. And there you have it—chicken and stock for curry with extra stock left over to use in any number of soups, sauces or stews.

For the chicken and stock

*1 3- to 3½-lb. chicken cut into
    6 pieces*

Water

1 large carrot, scraped

1 large onion, peeled

2 or 3 cloves garlic

*Plus a few leafy celery tops
    and sprigs of parsley (if
    you have them on hand)*

½ tsp. salt

½ cup dry vermouth

For the curry

*1 medium-size onion, peeled
    and finely minced*

*1 medium-size crisp, tart
    apple, peeled, cored and
    finely minced*

3 tbs. butter

2 tbs. curry powder

2 tbs. flour

*2 cups chicken stock (see page
    18)*

¼ cup dry vermouth

½ cup sour cream

*Meat from 3- to 3½-lb.
    poached chicken, skinned,
    boned and diced*

Salt

Pepper

To prepare chicken and stock

Place chicken pieces in a large pot and cover with water; bring to a boil and skim surface of water until clear. Add all remaining ingredients, except vermouth. Lower heat and let simmer until chicken is sufficiently tender to easily remove meat from bone. Remove chicken pieces and allow to stand until cool enough to handle. Remove meat and skin from bone and return bones to stew pot. Add vermouth and allow stock to simmer for 1½ to 2 hours. Cool slightly. Strain. Refrigerate until all fat has risen to surface and congealed. Remove and discard fat. Store stock, covered, in refrigerator until ready to use.

To prepare curry

Sauté onion and apple in butter until onion is very tender and apple reduced to a pulp. Stir in curry powder, then flour. Cook, stirring several minutes. Slowly add stock, stirring as added. Cook, stirring often, until mixture is smooth and thick. Add diced chicken and sour cream, and continue to cook, stirring, until steamy hot. Season with salt and pepper and serve over just-cooked, hot white or brown rice.

Serves 4 to 6

Notes

Curry can be served without the usual accompaniments, but the flavor is heightened and brought out by chutney—and it becomes a party dish when you add small bowls of chopped, dry-roasted peanuts, minced green onion and parsley to sprinkle over each serving.

SAUTEED CHICKEN LIVERS

4 tbs. butter

2 tbs. green onion, minced
    (white part only)

1 clove garlic, peeled and
    minced

1 tbs. flour

1 cup homemade chicken
    stock, heated (see page
    18)

1 tbs. mild vegetable oil

1 lb. chicken livers, washed
    and patted thoroughly
    dry

Salt

Pepper

½ cup sweet (red) Doubonnet
    wine

1 tsp. tarragon or white wine
    vinegar

1 tbs. green onion tops,
    minced (optional)

2 tbs. parsley, minced
    (optional)

White rice

Homemade mango chutney
    (see page 172) or green
    pepper jelly (see page 174)

Melt 2 tbs. of the butter in a saucepan and add the minced onion and garlic. Sauté until limp. Stir in flour; when blended pour in the heated stock and cook, stirring, until thick and smooth. Remove from heat and reserve.

In a deep, heavy skillet heat the remaining butter with the oil until it begins to turn color. Add the chicken livers and sprinkle them liberally with salt and pepper. Cook, stirring, over medium heat until lightly browned but still slightly pink in center. Cut into one to make sure.

Remove the livers with a slotted spoon to a warm platter. Add the Doubonnet to the skillet, bring to a boil over high heat and cook, stirring until reduced by about half. Stir in the reserved sauce and cook, stirring until mixture returns to a full boil; add the chicken livers, reduce heat and simmer until heated thoroughly. Stir in vinegar and correct seasoning with salt and pepper.

Spoon over just-cooked rice and serve chutney or jelly as an accompaniment.

Serves 4 to 6

CHICKEN SALAD

2 cups poached chicken cut
into bite-size chunks (see
page 93)

NOTE: Don't overcook the chicken. It should come off the bone in large pieces that can be cut into chunks, not shredded.

2 cups celery, diced	*2 tbs. fresh lemon juice*
2 tbs. chives, minced	*2 tsp. curry powder*
1 cup seedless white grapes	*1/2 cup mayonnaise*
cut in half	*1/4 cup sour cream*

Combine chicken, celery, chives and grapes in a large bowl. Mix lemon juice, curry powder, mayonnaise and sour cream. Blend well. Pour over chicken and celery mixture and toss well to blend. Refrigerate 2 to 3 hours before serving.

Serves 6 to 8

Note

Like all mayonnaise mixtures this salad must stay cold. It will spoil quickly if not refrigerated.

GIBLET AND CORN
BREAD LOAF

This is a wonderfully good low-cost main dish, rich in protein from stock and the chicken or turkey livers and giblets.

Actually, this is my mother's Louisianna recipe for turkey stuffing, but—remembering how no one got enough dressing and there was always leftover turkey—I made it into a main course dish to be served hot with gravy and cranberry sauce, or to serve cold with broiled fresh peaches or pickled peaches. Add a big bowl of coleslaw, a deep-dish pie for dessert, and dinner is served for anyone lucky enough to be present.

1 or 2 chicken or turkey giblets	3 cups crumbled corn bread
1 carrot, peeled and chopped	(recipe follows)
2 cloves garlic, peeled and cut in half	2 cups chicken stock (see page 18)
2 cups water	2 eggs, lightly beaten
3 or 4 chicken or turkey livers	½ tsp. salt
2 tbs. butter	1 tsp. sugar
1 cup celery, finely minced	1 tsp. coarsely ground black
½ cup onion, finely minced	pepper

Place giblets in saucepan with carrot, garlic and water. Bring to a boil and cook over medium heat 30 to 40 minutes or until tender. Add livers to cooking liquid last 10 minutes of cooking. Set aside to cool.

Melt butter in a small saucepan, add minced celery and onion, and sauté over low heat until vegetables are soft and golden.

Preheat oven to 300°F.

Place corn bread crumbs in large mixing bowl, add stock and sautéed vegetables. Add chopped cooked liver and giblets (reserve liquid in which liver and giblets were cooked) and blend well. Pour into lightly greased, shallow baking dish and bake in preheated oven 30 to 40 minutes.

Cut into squares and serve with giblet gravy (recipe follows), or chill and serve as suggested above.

Serves 6

EASY CORN BREAD

3 tbs. butter   3 tsp. baking powder
1 cup flour   1 tsp. salt
1 cup cornmeal   1 egg
2 tbs. sugar   1 cup milk

Preheat oven to 350°F.

Melt butter in heavy skillet and place in oven to keep hot. Combine all dry ingredients and mix well. Beat the egg in a small bowl, add the milk and beat to blend. Pour egg-milk mixture into dry ingredients, mix only to blend. Pour hot melted butter in and stir in quickly. Pour into hot skillet and bake at once for 20 to 30 minutes or until firm and golden.

GIBLET GRAVY

2 tbs. butter   1 tbs. Worcestershire sauce
2 tbs. flour   Salt to taste
Strained liquid in which   Coarsely ground black pepper
    giblets were cooked; add   to taste
    sufficient chicken stock to
    make 2 cups liquid

Melt the butter in a small saucepan, add the flour and cook, stirring, over very low heat for 3 to 4 minutes. Don't undercook or flour will taste "raw." Slowly add cooking liquid and stock; continue to cook, stirring, until gravy is thick and smooth. Add seasonings, stir to blend and serve hot.

chapter five

Fish for Gourmets

FISH COOKERY

Fish cookery is a wonderful art to acquire, not only because fish is nutritious but because whether bought or caught it's still relatively inexpensive in comparison to meat. Rich in vitamins and minerals, it is also filling, while at the same time, with very little effort it can be true gourmet fare.

Rule number one for cooking any and all fish (seafood too) is don't overcook. Overcooking robs fish of its delicious juices and makes the texture dry.

The fat content of fish tells you the best method of preparation. As a rule fatty fish are most desirable for broiling or baking because their fat content will prevent them from becoming dry. Lean fish is preferred by many for poaching or steaming because their flesh is firm. However, all fish may be cooked by any basic method if allowances are made for the fat content. Lean fish may be broiled or baked if basted frequently.

Cleaning a Fish

Scales can be removed with a knife or a scaling tool which is available in most tackle shops. Wash the fish and lay it on a flat surface with newspaper under it. Starting with the tail, remove the scales by holding the blade of the knife vertically and scraping toward the head. Wash the fish again to remove any loose scales. Fold back the top sheet of paper in half to give a surface free of loose scales. For small- to medium-size fish, cut the underside of the fish from the vent to the head, remove the entrails (intestines) and cut off the head. Cook whole.

For very large fish, clean as above. Then cut the fish crosswise into steaks about 1-inch thick. To prepare fillets cut the fish through to the backbone just behind the small fin near the head. Cut along the backbone and over the rib bones. Lift the fillet off, and repeat on other side. Roll the remaining parts of the fish in the newspaper and discard.

Buying fish

What to ask for and what you will get

Whole or round fish: as they come from the water.
Drawn: whole fish with only the entrails removed.
Dressed and pan dressed: scaled with entrails, head, tail and fins removed.
Steaks: a cross section from large dressed fish.
Fillet: the side of the fish cut lengthwise away from the bone.

When buying a whole fish with skin, bone and tail included, allow 1 lb. for each ½ lb. of edible fish.

to make sure it's fresh

The eyes should be bright, clear and bulging.
The gills should be reddish or pink, clean and fresh smelling.
The scales should be bright, shiny and tight to the skin.
The flesh should be firm and should spring back when pressed.
There should be no strong or unpleasant odor.
Buy ¾ lb. of dressed or pan-dressed fish for each serving; ½ lb. of fillets or steaks.

To insure fresh fish stays fresh until cooked, rush it home and store in a covered dish in refrigerator. Cook within 24 hours.

Now for a few menus. As with cheese and egg entrees, fish is on the light side, so balance your meal planning with potatoes, rice or an interesting bread and a good dessert.

A FESTIVE BUT EASY PARTY MENU

(asterisk refers to recipe in this book)

JELLIED GAZPACHO SALAD *
(Served as a first course
with Mayonnaise)
BAKED WHOLE FISH *
TINY NEW POTATOES
ROLLED IN BUTTER AND CHOPPED PARSLEY
CHILLED DRY WHITE WINE
CRÊPES SUZETTES *
COFFEE

3 SUMMER MENUS

STUFFED BAKED TROUT *
RICE
BABY LIMA BEANS
DRY WHITE WINE
SPONGE CAKE * WITH
STRAWBERRIES AND SOUR CREAM
COFFEE

ITALIAN FISH STEW *
CRUSTY ITALIAN BREAD
DRY RED WINE
BAKED PEACHES IN RED WINE
MADELEINES *
COFFEE

BREADED FISH FILLETS *
CORN PUDDING *
SAUTÉED ZUCCHINI AND TOMATOES ITALIAN STYLE *
COLD BEER
RICE CUSTARD * WITH
PEACH PURÉE *
COFFEE

WINTER MENUS

FISH AND POTATO BAKE *
APPLE AND CABBAGE COLESLAW *
COLD BEER
APPLESAUCE CAKE *
COFFEE

ORIENTAL SALT-BROILED FISH *
STUFFED BAKED POTATOES *
DRY WHITE WINE
PARISIENNE CARROTS AND ONIONS *
PEANUT BUTTER PIE *
COFFEE

PAUPIETTES DE SOLE *
RICE
SPINACH SALAD
WITH PORK BITS *
CHILLED DRY WHITE WINE
BUDGET-BAKE BANANAS *
COFFEE

FILLET OF SOLE AU GRATIN *
ROASTED POTATOES

CHILLED DRY WHITE WINE
GRAPEFRUIT SALAD WITH
VINAIGRETTE DRESSING *
INDIAN PUDDING *

POACHED FISH

Poaching fish is easy. It tastes great, is inexpensive and can be, if you desire it, quite a gourmet feast.

Use any small white fish such as whiting, halibut or cod.

Make Court Bouillon (recipe follows). Add fish and let cook at just below simmering point until flesh flakes easily when touched with a fork. Remove fish (use one, or if fish is large, two slotted spatulas to remove fish) to a heated serving platter. Serve hot with Sauce Velouté (recipe follows) or chill fish and serve with mayonnaise or sour cream mixed with peeled and minced cucumber and/or green onion.

COURT BOUILLON

1 lb. fish bones and heads
3 qts. water
1 tbs. butter
1 thick slice lemon
1 thick slice onion
1 clove garlic, peeled

1 carrot, scraped and sliced
1 bay leaf
1 cup dry red or white wine or
        dry vermouth (optional)
1 tsp. salt
4 to 6 peppercorns

Combine ingredients in a large, shallow pan. Bring to a boil; then reduce heat and let simmer for about 30 minutes. Use a slotted spoon to remove vegetables, fish bones and heads.

SAUCE VELOUTÉ

2 tbs. butter
2 tbs. flour
2 cups strained stock used to
    poach fish, heated
Salt

Pepper
A little sour cream or heavy
    cream or a bit of grated
    mild cheese (optional)

In a saucepan, melt butter over low heat and stir in flour. Cook, stirring until well blended and smooth. Add heated stock and first beat, then stir with whisk until sauce is thick and smooth. Season with salt and pepper. If desired, just before removing from heat stir in 2 to 3 tbs. sour cream or heavy cream, or 1 to 2 tbs. grated Swiss cheese.

Makes about 2 cups sauce.

DEVILED BROILED FISH

4 or 6 small whole fish,
    cleaned and heads
    removed; or 4 to 6 thick
    fish fillets
4 tbs. water
2 tbs. butter or margarine

Paprika
½ cup mayonnaise
1 tbs. dry mustard
1 tbs. lemon juice
½ tsp. salt

Preheat oven to 350°F. Place fish or fish fillets in baking dish. Pour in water. Dot with butter. Bake uncovered for 15 to 20 minutes, depending on thickness of fish.

Remove from oven.

Combine remaining ingredients and blend well. Spread over surface of fish. Place under broiler heat until topping is bubbly hot and flecked with brown.

Serves 4 to 6

ITALIAN FISH STEW

Any fresh or salt water fish will do nicely. Buy the least expensive available, as all are equally good: sea bass, skate, red snapper, cod, or even catfish, which has been commercially developed into a really great and inexpensive fish.

4 lbs. cleaned fish with heads
4 cups water
¼ tsp. salt
¼ tsp. pepper
1 small onion, peeled and
    quartered
2 to 3 sprigs parsley
½ tsp. mixed Italian herbs

1 clove garlic, minced
1 tbs. flour
½ cup oil
2 tbs. butter
1 1-lb. can Italian-style
    tomatoes with basil
½ cup dry white wine

Remove heads, trim the fish and cut it into ½-inch slices.

Place heads and trimmings in a heavy pot with the water, salt, pepper, onion, parsley, herbs and garlic. Bring to a boil, then lower heat and let simmer for about 30 minutes. Strain and set aside.

Wipe fish slices dry and dredge with flour. Rub flour into each piece and then shake off excess.

Heat the oil in a soup kettle. Add fish pieces a few at a time and brown them quickly over medium-high heat. Remove as browned.

When all fish is browned, pour cooking oil from pot and add butter. Return fish to pot; add reserved stock, tomatoes and wine. Simmer for about 15 minutes. Serve with crusty Italian bread and chilled white wine.

Serves 6

ITALIAN FISH CHOWDER

⅓ cup salad oil
2 cloves garlic, peeled and
    finely minced
1 purple Italian onion, peeled
    and minced
½ cup celery, finely minced
½ cup carrots, finely minced
¼ cup parsley, chopped
1 tsp. mixed Italian seasoning
1 cup dry white wine

1 cup water
1 1-lb. can tomatoes
3 lbs. fish fillets (sole, flounder
    or bass)
½ tsp. salt
½ tsp. coarsely ground black
    pepper
6 thick slices Italian bread,
    lightly toasted

Heat the oil in a deep, heavy soup pot, add the garlic and onion and sauté over very low heat until vegetables are soft and golden. Add all remaining ingredients, except fish, salt and pepper. Stir to blend. Cook over low heat, stirring frequently, for 15 to 20 minutes. Cut fish into bite-size chunks and add to liquid in the pot; cook for an additional 10 to 15 minutes or until fish flakes easily with a fork. Stir in salt and pepper. Serve very hot in soup bowls with a slice of the toasted Italian bread on top of each serving.

Serves 6

PAUPIETTES DE SOLES

Add this to your repertoire of classic French dishes from the late, great Le Pavillon restaurant. For all its glorious taste it is as light on the budget as it is on your fork and a lovely choice for a perfect dinner party. The trick here is the sparing but definite use of wine and butter with inexpensive ingredients. After all, fillets of fish are one of your best buys. Serve with small, boiled new potatoes peeled and sprinkled with parsley, and a glass of chilled white wine.

5 tbs. butter
½ cup chives, finely minced
½ cup celery, finely minced
½ onion, finely minced
8 fillets of sole
2 eggs

1½ cups milk
1 cup fine, dry bread crumbs
2 tbs. flour
½ cup dry white wine
½ tsp. salt
2 tbs. Parmesan cheese

Melt 2 tbs. of the butter in a deep, heavy skillet over very low heat and sauté the finely minced vegetables in the butter, stirring constantly, until they are soft and golden. Spread each sole fillet with the vegetable mixture, roll up and fasten with a toothpick. Beat the eggs lightly with ½ cup of the milk and dip each fish roll first in egg mixture (reserve leftover egg mixture) and then in bread crumbs. Allow to dry slightly. Melt the remaining butter in the skillet in which the vegetables were cooked and brown the fish rolls a few at a time over medium heat. As the rolls are browned transfer to an oven-proof shallow casserole. When all are browned, add the flour to the butter remaining in the pan and, if necessary, add an additional 1 tbs. butter. Cook, stirring, over low heat for 2 or 3 minutes, slowly add the remaining cup of milk and cook until sauce begins to thicken. Add reserved egg mixture and wine; continue to cook over very low heat until sauce is thick and smooth. Pour over fish rolls, sprinkle with Parmesan cheese and bake in preheated 350°F. oven until bubbly hot and fish flakes easily with the prongs of a fork.

Serves 4 to 8 (depending on how hungry everyone is)

BAKED WHOLE FISH

1 4-lb. *whole fish, scaled and
    cleaned (bluefish, trout,
    snapper, striped bass,
    etc.)*
Salt
Pepper
1 tbs. *butter, soft, room
    temperature*
2 cups *water*
1 medium-size *onion, peeled
    and quartered*
1 clove *garlic, peeled and split
    lengthwise*
3 or 4 *thin strips of lemon peel*
*Plus any or all of the
    following*

¼ to ⅓ cup *mushroom
    stems, chopped*
1 to 2 tbs. *green onion tops,
    minced*
1 to 2 tbs. *parsley stems,
    minced*
2 or 4 *ends of fresh tomatoes*
1 or 2 *leafy celery tops*
½ cup *dry white wine*

For the sauce
1 tbs. *butter*
1 tbs. *flour*
1 cup *liquid used in baking
    fish*
1 tbs. *parsley or green onion
    tops, minced*

To prepare the fish

Wash fish inside and out, blot dry, sprinkle with salt and pepper and rub on both sides with butter. Place in a shallow baking dish. Refrigerate while preparing stock.

Place water in a saucepan with onion, garlic and lemon peel. Bring to a boil, then lower heat and let simmer until reduced by about half. Add wine.

Preheat oven to 400°F.

Strain stock and pour over fish. Bake in preheated oven for 35 minutes, basting frequently.

To prepare the sauce

While fish bakes, melt the butter in the top half of a double boiler and stir in flour. Cook, stirring often, over (not in) simmering water until mixture turns a deep gold in color and develops a sweet nutlike fragrance. Keep hot over hot water.

When fish is baked transfer it to a heated platter (use two spatulas for easy handling) and keep warm.

Place butter mixture over direct heat. When bubbly add, all at once, 1 cup of the hot liquid used in baking the fish and stir rapidly with a whisk to a thick smooth sauce. Pour over fish and sprinkle with chopped parsley (or green onion) and serve at once.

Serves 6

FISH AND POTATO BAKE

2 2-lb. mackerel or red
    snapper (or any other
    firm white fish, cleaned,
    with or without tails and
    heads—as you prefer; but
    if you just trim the tail
    and leave the head intact
    the flavor will be better)
Salt
1 tsp. onion, shredded
Juice from one lemon

1 cup soft bread crumbs (made
    in blender from French-
    or Italian-style bread)
1 tbs. parsley, finely chopped
4 tbs. butter
2 large California white
    potatoes, peeled and
    sliced
Freshly ground black pepper
Salt
1 cup water

Preheat oven to 350°F.

Wash the fish under cold running water and pat them dry. Sprinkle lightly inside and out with salt.

In a small bowl combine the shredded onion, lemon juice, bread crumbs and parsley.

Melt the butter and pour half of it over bread crumb mixture.

Spread the potato slices evenly in the bottom of a well-buttered baking dish. Sprinkle lightly with salt and pepper. Place fish on top of potatoes. Pour the water into the bottom of the baking dish. Sprinkle the top of each fish evenly with the bread-crumb mixture and pour the remaining melted butter slowly over them.

Bake in preheated oven for 30 minutes until the fish tests done and the potatoes are tender.

Serve from the baking dish.

Serves 4 to 6

BREADED
FISH FILLETS

1½ lbs. fresh fish fillets (any
type fish will do nicely,
just be sure it's fresh)
½ cup mayonnaise

1 tsp. salt
1 cup fine, dry bread crumbs
2 tbs. butter, melted

Preheat oven to very hot 500°F.

Cut the fillets into serving pieces. Coat each with mayonnaise. Sprinkle with salt and roll in bread crumbs. Place in a single layer in a well-buttered baking dish and pour the butter evenly over them. Bake on the top shelf of the preheated oven for 15 minutes.

Serve with lemon wedges.

Serves 4 to 6

STUFFED BAKED TROUT

This is a lovely way to cook trout. It's a summer time recipe, though, needing the taste that only fresh summer vegetables can give.

6 small to medium-size trout
3 tbs. butter
½ cup green onions, finely
minced
1 cup fine, dry bread crumbs
½ tsp. salt

½ tsp. pepper
¼ cup parsley, finely minced
2 cups stewed fresh tomatoes
½ cup dry white wine or dry
vermouth

Preheat oven to 350°F.

Wash the trout and pat dry. Place open side up in a shallow baking dish. Melt the butter in a heavy saucepan, add the minced green onions and sauté until onions are soft and golden. Add the parsley, bread crumbs, seasoning and just enough of the stewed tomatoes to hold the ingredients together. Stuff the fish with this mixture. Combine remaining stewed tomatoes with wine. Blend well and pour over fish. Cover the baking dish and bake for 25 to 30 minutes. Uncover during last 5 minutes of baking.

Serve very hot with freshly cooked rice.

Serves 6

FILLET OF SOLE AU GRATIN

4 fillets of sole
½ tsp. salt
¼ cup salad oil

½ cup sour cream
½ cup grated domestic Swiss
   cheese

Place the fillets in a shallow nonmetal casserole, sprinkle with salt and pour oil over surface. Allow to stand for 15 to 20 minutes. Drain oil from fish and discard. Place fish under preheated broiler and cook until fish is firm and lightly browned. Remove from heat, cover with sour cream and then with cheese. Return to broiler for 5 or 6 minutes or until cheese is melted.

Serve at once with boiled new potatoes and fresh green peas.

Serves 4

ORIENTAL SALT-BROILED FISH

This is such an easy method of preparing fish that a recipe is really not needed. Do not, however, dismiss it as too uninteresting or dull. Fish broiled in this way is so utterly delicious that despite its low cost you will rate it gourmet.

For each serving
1 fish fillet—¼ to ⅓ lb. per
   serving—(any fish with
   skin left on)

Salt
Soy sauce

About ½ hour before cooking remove fish from refrigerator and sprinkle lightly on both sides with salt. Let stand at room temperature; when ready to broil place skin side up in a lightly greased, shallow baking dish. Place about 4 inches under medium-high broiler heat. Broil about 5 minutes. Turn with a spatula and continue to broil until flesh flakes easily and fish puffs up a bit. Exact timing depends on thickness of fish, but it usually takes no more than 10 minutes total broiling time.

Sprinkle each fillet lightly with soy sauce just before serving.

I like fish prepared in this way with Chinese fried rice, but plain boiled rice is a fine accompaniment when prepared in this way:

Place 3 cups cold cooked rice in a shallow baking dish and mix in sufficient soy sauce to coat the grains. Stir in about ½ cup finely chopped celery. Bake in a preheated 350°F. oven, stirring occasionally, until heated and dry.

chapter six

From the Dairy: Egg and Cheese Dishes

EGG AND CHEESE DISHES

The dairy counter can be the source of an endless variety of interesting, easy and, nicest of all, inexpensive main courses. Needless to say, eggs and cheese are top sources of protein, but the really important point is they taste marvelous. Here are a few menus that are proven favorites of my family and friends. I think you will find them just as satisfying as those centered around meat or chicken and, in fact, a wonderful change of pace from the monotony of everyday meals. The one point to remember about menus planned around such fairly light entrees is to balance them with slightly more substantial vegetables, such as corn or lima beans, or add hot rolls and/or an interesting dessert. Nor do these additions make for more work or more expense. Take a look at the sample menus shown—they are all variations on this theme. I hope you find them helpful in adding interest and variety to the day-to-day chore of choosing what's for dinner.

SUMMER

(asterisks refer to recipe to be found in this book)

EASY CHEESE CROQUETTES
WITH CREOLE SAUCE *
STEAMED LIMA BEANS
HOT HOMEMADE ROLLS
COLD BEER
SUMMER SNOW PUDDING *
COFFEE

FRESH TOMATO-CUCUMBER SHRUB *
CHEESE TIMBALES *
CREAMED FRESH PEAS OR BROCCOLI
HOT HOMEMADE ROLLS *
CHILLED WHITE WINE
PEACH DEEP-DISH PIE
WITH EASY CRACKER CRUST *

VICHYSSOISE *
INDIVIDUAL TOMATO QUICHES *
CORN ON THE COB
CHILLED WHITE WINE
TAPIOCA CUSTARD * WITH
FRESH BLUEBERRIES

CORN CHOWDER *
GOUGERE *
DRY RED WINE
SPINACH SALAD WITH PORK BITS *
SPONGE CAKE *
PEACH PUREE * AND SOUR CREAM

WINTER

DEVILED EGGS *
COLD BEER
CANNED POTATO STICKS
DEEP-DISH APPLE PIE
WITH CRUMB TOPPING
COFFEE

POTATO-CHEESE SOUFFLÉ *
PARISIENNE CARROTS AND ONIONS *
CHILLED WHITE WINE
BROILED GRAPEFRUIT
"ANYTHING GOES" COOKIES *
COFFEE

CURRIED EGGS *
COLD BEER
BEET AND ORANGE SALAD *
INDIAN PUDDING
COFFEE

DUTCH-KITCHEN CHEESE
AND VEGETABLE PIE *
COLD BEER
RED-HOT TOMATO CHUTNEY *
HOMEMADE HOT ROLLS *
ORANGE AND GRAPEFRUIT SECTIONS
WITH SHREDDED COCONUT *
COFFEE

CURRIED EGGS

6 to 8 hard-cooked eggs
4 tbs. butter
1 small tart apple, peeled,
    cored and finely chopped
1 small white onion, peeled
    and finely minced

2 tbs. curry powder
2 tbs. flour
1½ cups milk
2 tbs. parsley, minced
Chutney (see pages 172
    and 173)

Slice the eggs and place them in a double layer, each layer slightly overlapping, in a buttered, long, shallow baking dish. Set aside while preparing sauce.

Melt the butter in a saucepan over low heat. Add the apple and onion. Cook, stirring, until onion is limp and apple is reduced to a puree, about 10 minutes. Stir in first the curry powder, then flour and stir until smooth. Slowly add milk, stirring as added. Cook, stirring, until sauce is thick and smooth.

Pour sauce over eggs and place in a preheated 350°F. oven until bubbly hot. Sprinkle with parsley and serve at once with homemade chutney.

Serves 4 to 6

PUFFED-CHEESE AND HAM OMELET

1 medium onion, peeled and
    very finely chopped
1 large raw potato, peeled and
    very finely chopped
1 tbs. vegetable shortening
Salt
4 eggs, beaten

¼ cup grated Swiss cheese, or
    2 tbs. grated Parmesan
    cheese
¼ cup lean (leftover) baked or
    braised ham, chopped
    (optional)
1 tbs. butter, melted

The original recipe called for Mancheyo, a mellow, mild and very good cheese imported from Spain—use it, of course, if you can find and afford it—but natural Swiss cheese or Parmesan cheese are equally good substitutes and far less expensive.

Don't substitute butter or margarine for the vegetable shortening or the omelet will stick.

Both onion and potato must be chopped very fine.

Preheat broiler oven to high.

Heat shortening in a 9- to 10-inch skillet. Add onion and potato and cook over low heat, turning them frequently and chopping them still more with the tip of a spatula as they cook. When potato and onion are very soft, sprinkle lightly with salt.

Combine beaten eggs, grated cheese and, if desired, chopped ham. Pour over potatoes and vegetables. Shake the pan to distribute eggs evenly, but do not stir. Cook over medium heat until eggs are "set" on bottom. Pour melted butter over surface and place about 3 inches under broiler heat until puffed and lightly browned. Turn out onto a round platter or cut in wedges and serve from the pan.

Serves 4

HARD-COOKED EGGS
FLORENTINE

2 lbs. fresh spinach	Salt
2 tbs. butter	Pepper
2 tbs. flour	8 hard-cooked eggs, sliced
1½ cups chicken stock, heated (see page 18)	½ cup grated cheddar cheese

Wash spinach thoroughly under cold running water. Remove and discard tough stems. Place in a large skillet with only the water that clings to the leaves. Cover, place over moderate heat and let steam for about 10 minutes or until limp. Drain thoroughly. Chop. Place in the bottom of a buttered, long, shallow baking dish.

Melt the butter in a saucepan and stir in the flour. Cook,

stirring, several minutes. Add the heated stock and stir with a whisk to a smooth thick sauce. Season with salt and pepper.

Pour half the sauce over spinach. Cover with the sliced, hard-cooked eggs.

Stir the cheese into the remaining sauce (it doesn't have to melt completely) and pour over the eggs.

Bake for about 10 minutes in preheated oven or only until bubbly hot.

Serve with sliced buttered toast.

Serves 4

Notes

2 or 3 tbs. of dry sherry added to the sauce before adding the cheese gives this dish a luxury taste.

DEVILED EGGS

4 *English muffins*	1 *tsp. Worcestershire sauce*
1 *cup chili sauce* (*see page 63*)	*Salt*
1 *tbs. cider vinegar*	*Pepper*
1 *tbs. butter*	8 *hard-cooked eggs, sliced*

Tear muffins apart and place under broiler to heat until lightly toasted.

In a saucepan combine chili sauce, vinegar, butter and Worcestershire sauce. Stir over low heat to boiling. Spoon a little of the mixture over each half muffin on serving plates. Cover each with slices of the hard-cooked egg. Spoon remaining sauce over and serve at once.

Serves 4

EGGS BAKED IN RED RICE

½ small green pepper, seeded
    and finely chopped
1 medium-size onion, peeled
    and minced
2 tbs. butter
1 cup long grain rice
1 cup tomato juice, room
    temperature

1 cup chicken stock or water,
    room temperature
½ tsp salt
6 eggs
½ cup grated natural Swiss
    cheese

In a saucepan sauté green pepper and onion in 1 tbs. of the butter over low heat until vegetables are limp. Add remaining butter; when melted, stir in rice and cook, stirring, until each grain is coated with butter. Add tomato juice and stock or water. Bring to a full boil, then lower heat, cover and let simmer until all liquid is absorbed. Spoon into a buttered, long, shallow baking dish.

Make 6 indentations in rice; break an egg into each. Sprinkle cheese on top. Cover and bake in a preheated 400°F. oven until eggs are set, about 15 minutes.

Serves 6

Notes

Add broiled peach halves, crusty rolls and dry white wine to this one. It's great.

FRITTATA

1 tbs. vegetable oil
1 tbs. butter
4 green onions, minced
1 cup boiled potatoes, diced
½ cup cooked green peas
5 eggs

½ tsp. salt
¼ tsp. coarsely ground black
    pepper
2 lbs. freshly grated Parmesan
    cheese

Adjust broiler rack to about 4 inches below heat. Preheat broiler to 500°F.

Melt butter with oil in a heavy 9-inch skillet (with a heat-proof handle) over medium heat.

Add onions and sauté until soft. Add potatoes and cook until heated thoroughly (use a spatula to turn and stir often as they heat). Stir in peas. Spread potatoes and vegetables evenly over bottom of skillet. Remove from heat.

Beat eggs with salt, pepper and grated cheese until blended. Return skillet to medium heat. Pour egg mixture over potato mixture, tilting skillet back and forth to distribute evenly. Do NOT stir. Cook only until eggs at bottom of skillet have set. Transfer skillet to preheated broiler. Broil until the frittata is puffed and firm and golden with flecks of brown.

Cut into pie-shaped wedges. Lift wedges from skillet with a spatula onto warm serving plate.

Serves 4

BASIC CHEESE SOUFFLÉ

Most recipes for cheese soufflé call for such precise ingredients; actually, almost any liquid and any natural cheese may be used.

3 tbs. butter

3 tbs. flour

1 cup milk, room temperature
  or ½ cup clear, fat-free chicken stock and ½ cup milk
  or ½ cup beer and ½ cup cream
  or ¾ cup milk and ¼ cup dry white wine.

½ tsp. salt

1 cup shredded or grated cheese—mild or sharp cheddar, natural Swiss, Provolone or fontina
  or ½ cup grated Swiss and ½ cup grated Parmesan;
  or ¾ cup American or brick and ¼ cup Parmesan or Romano. (The only cheese to avoid are "processed" cheeses of any kind; "natural" cheese is what you need and must have to prepare a never-fail, always-good soufflé.)

6 eggs, separated

Preheat oven to 350°F.

Make a cream sauce; melt butter, stir in flour and cook over very low heat until mixture is golden in color and has a nutlike aroma. Remove from heat, slowly pour in milk (or other liquid), stirring as added. Add salt; return pan to low heat and cook, stirring, until smooth. Add cheese and stir to a thick sauce.

Remove from heat, cool slightly. Then add egg yolks, one at a time, beating with a whisk after each addition.

Beat egg whites until stiff.

Stir about 2 tbs. of the beaten egg whites into the sauce mixture, then gently fold in remaining egg whites. Pour into a well-buttered 1½ quart soufflé mold. Bake 30 to 35 minutes in preheated oven until soufflé is high, puffed and golden.

Serve at once.

Serves 4

Variations

Add to liquid 1 tsp. Worcestershire sauce, a dash of hot pepper sauce, ½- to ¾-cup chopped, minced ham (baked or braised), or flaked, cooked fish or chopped seafood.

Fold into cream sauce before adding egg whites, ½- to ¾-cup cooked, well-drained chopped spinach or tiny green peas or any other well-chopped, cooked, leftover vegetable.

EASY CHEESE CROQUETTES
WITH CREOLE SAUCE

½ lb. Swiss cheese, coarsely
    grated
½ lb. American cheese,
    coarsely grated
4 tbs. butter, room
    temperature
1 tbs. prepared mustard

1 tsp. salt
1 tbs. finely minced parsley or
    green onions or both
2 eggs, beaten
2 cups cracker crumbs
3 tbs. butter

Mix together all but shortening and sauce. Shape into croquettes. Chill until firm.

Fry over low heat in butter until lightly browned on both sides.

Serves 6

DUTCH KITCHEN CHEESE
AND VEGETABLE PIE

3 cups of ½-inch bread
   squares, lightly toasted
1 large tomato, thinly sliced
1 1-lb. can mixed vegetables
2 cups (½ lb.) natural Swiss
   cheese, shredded

3 eggs lightly beaten
½ tsp. dry mustard
1 ⅓ cups milk
½ tsp. salt
2 to 3 dashes hot pepper sauce
   (see page 179)

Arrange toasted bread squares in the bottom of a lightly buttered 9-inch pie plate (or a square baking dish). Cover with tomato slices. Top first with vegetables, then cheese.

Beat eggs with mustard until blended. Add milk, salt and pepper sauce. Blend and pour over surface of pie. Let stand 30 minutes. Bake in a 350°F. preheated oven until firm, 30 to 40 minutes.

Serves 4 to 6

CHEESE TIMBALES

¾ cup milk
¾ cup chicken stock (see page
   18)
   or 1½ cups milk
   or 1 cup stock and ½ cup
   heavy cream

1 cup grated cheese—mild
   cheddar, American, brick
   or Swiss
½ tsp. salt
¼ tsp. white pepper
4 eggs

Preheat oven to 325°F.

Heat milk with stock; add cheese, stir until melted and mixture is smooth.

Remove from heat; season with salt and pepper. Beat in eggs one at a time.

Pour into 4 to 6 well-buttered individual molds or custard cups. Place molds (or cups) on a rack in a pan of hot (not boiling) water and bake in preheated oven until firm, about 20 minutes.

Remove from pan of water and let stand about 5 minutes. Run a knife around the inside of each mold. Invert and turn out onto serving plates.

Serve with creamed peas, or steamed broccoli or spinach.

Serves 6

Notes

If desired, add ½- to 1-cup chopped cooked vegetables; broccoli or cauliflower, well-drained steamed spinach, sautéed mushrooms.

QUICHE AND VARIATIONS

CLASSIC QUICHE

1 9-inch unbaked pastry shell	8 oz. Swiss cheese, shredded
½ cup lean (leftover, baked)	4 eggs, well beaten
ham, diced	1½ cups milk

Preheat oven to 450°F.

Bake pastry shell in preheated oven for 8 minutes only. Remove from oven, reduce heat to 325°F.

Cool partially baked shell. Combine ham and cheese and place in pie shell.

Combine eggs and milk. Blend well and pour over mixture.

Bake in 325°F. oven for 35 to 40 minutes or until custard is firm. Let stand about 10 minutes before serving.

Serves 6

ONION QUICHE
(Less Expensive)

2 tbs. butter
½ cup onion, minced
3 eggs, lightly beaten
1¾ cup milk
2 to 3 dashes hot pepper sauce
    (see page 179)

½ tsp. salt
¼ cup grated Parmesan
    cheese
1 9-inch pie shell, partially
    baked (see Classic Quiche
    page 122)

Preheat oven to 325°F.

Melt the butter in a small skillet over low heat; add onions and cook, stirring often, until very soft.

Combine eggs and milk and blend well; season with hot pepper sauce and salt. Stir in cheese.

Sprinkle sautéed onion in bottom of pie shell. Pour egg mixture over.

Place in preheated oven and bake 30 to 40 minutes or until custard is firm.

Let stand 10 minutes before serving.

Serves 6

INDIVIDUAL
TOMATO QUICHES

6 medium tomatoes
6 tbs. lean ham from leftover
    baked or braised ham,
    minced
½ cup sour cream

2 eggs
2 tbs. grated Parmesan cheese
¼ tsp. pepper
¼ tsp. salt

Preheat oven to 400°F.

Wash tomatoes, cut a thin, horizontal slice from each and carefully hollow out centers, reserving pulp for another use (soup, stews, sauces, etc.). Place in shallow baking dish. Put 1 tbs. minced ham in each.

In a small bowl, with a fork beat sour cream with eggs, grated cheese, salt and pepper until combined. Use to fill tomatoes.

Bake 20 minutes or until filling is firm. Serve hot.

Serves 6

CHEESE STRATA

*8 slices day-old, firm white
    bread*
*½ lb. mild cheddar cheese,
    crumbled*
4 eggs

¼ tsp. dry mustard
2½ cups milk
½ cup dry white wine
½ tsp. salt
Paprika

Trim crusts from 5 slices of the bread; cut in half diagonally. Use crusts and remaining three slices of untrimmed bread to cover the bottom of an 8- or 9-inch square baking dish. Top with cheese. Arrange the 10 trimmed triangles in two slightly overlapping rows over cheese.

Beat eggs with mustard. Blend in milk and wine; add salt. Pour over bread and cheese. Cover and let stand 1 hour at room temperature or for several hours in refrigerator.

Bake in a preheated 325°F. oven for 1 hour or until knife inserted in center comes out clean.

Let stand about 5 minutes before serving.

Serves 6

GOUGERE

I discovered gougere several years ago and it has since become my favorite mainstay for a luncheon or supper dish whenever the budget is under a particular strain. Preceded by a hot or cold soup, depending on the season, and accompanied by an inexpensive spinach salad briskly flavored by crisp salt-pork chips, it's a delectable meal especially if you add a glass of red wine.

Gougere makes use of the classic French pâté à chou, rarely used in this country except for cream puffs. It sounds a little complicated, but the doing takes less time than the telling and the results are so spectacular the temptation is to just go on making them all day.

½ cup butter (1 stick) cut into small pieces	1½ tsps. homemade mustard (see page 178)
1 cup water	1½ tsps. salt
1 cup flour (unsifted)	1 cup Swiss cheese, coarsely grated
4 eggs	

Preheat oven to 450°F.

Generously grease a large cookie sheet with oil or butter and sprinkle with flour. Shake to distribute flour evenly. Shake out excess flour.

Place the butter and water in a 2-quart saucepan and bring to a rolling boil over high heat. When butter is completely melted, remove from heat and dump in flour all at once. With a large wooden spoon quickly mix the flour and water mixture until it is the consistency of mashed potatoes; then return the pan to the stove. Over moderate heat beat and mix the dough vigorously until it becomes a smooth mass that moves all together with the spoon. Remove the pan from the heat. Before the paste begins to cool, make an indentation in it with the back of a tablespoon, break an egg into it and quickly begin to beat. At first the paste will break into moist, doughy strands, but continue to beat vigorously until the strands come together and form a solid mass. At that point follow the same procedure with the second egg, and when the dough is solid again repeat with the third egg and then the fourth, making sure the dough is a solid mass before adding each egg. After the last egg is beaten in the dough should be smooth and shiny and fall lazily off the lifted spoon and back into the pan.

Beat in the seasonings and the cheese. Drop by spoonfulls on the prepared cookie sheet in circles to form two (not touching) rings. Bake on center shelf of preheated 450°F. oven for 10 minutes; then immediately lower heat to 350°F. and bake an additional 10 minutes; lower heat again, this time to 325°F., and bake for a final 20 minutes.

The gougeres should be nicely puffed and a golden brown. Serve immediately or let remain in the turned off oven (with door slightly ajar) up to 30 minutes. If you do this, pierce the gougeres in several places with the point of a small sharp knife to allow steam to escape and to prevent them from getting soggy.

Serves 8 to 10

POTATO-CHEESE SOUFFLÉ

4 large potatoes
½ cup milk heated with 1 tbs.
    butter
½ tsp. salt
⅛ tsp. pepper
½ cup creamy cottage cheese,
    room temperature

¼ cup sharp cheddar cheese,
    grated
2 egg yolks, well beaten
2 egg whites

Preheat oven to 350°F.

Boil potatoes in water to cover, until done. Peel and mash with hot milk and butter until smooth. Add salt and pepper. Beat in cottage cheese, cheddar cheese and egg yolks.

Beat egg whites until stiff and carefully fold into potato mixture.

Turn into an ungreased 1-quart soufflé mold and bake in preheated oven for about 1 hour or until well puffed and lightly browned.

Serves 6

Notes

To cut the cost of this dish substitute homemade chicken stock for milk or use reconstituted dry skim milk.

WELSH RAREBIT CASSEROLE
WITH TOMATOES

8 slices firm, fresh white bread	*2 egg yolks*
4 thick slices fresh tomato	*1 to 2 tsp. Worcestershire*
Sugar	*sauce*
Salt	*3 to 4 dashes Tabasco sauce*
2 tbs. butter	*½ to 1 tsp. Dijon-type*
2 tsp. flour	*mustard (hot) (see page*
1 cup flat beer or ale	*178)*
½ lb. sharp cheddar cheese,	*Salt, if needed*
shredded	

Trim crust from bread (save for bread crumbs) and toast lightly. Place tomato slices in a shallow baking dish and sprinkle very lightly with sugar and salt. Bake in a preheated 350°F. oven for about 10 minutes. Remove and set aside.

Preheat oven to broil.

Melt the butter in a 2- to 3-quart enamel or stainless steel saucepan over moderate heat and stir in the flour. When blended, slowly add the beer, stirring as added. Now handful by handful, add the cheese, stirring until it has dissolved after each addition, until all is added and the rarebit is thick and smooth.

Off the heat, beat in the egg yolks, then season with Worcestershire sauce, tabasco sauce and mustard. Taste and add salt if desired.

Place one slice of toast in the bottom of 4 individual shallow, oval au gratin (baking) dishes. Over each place a slice of tomato. Spoon some of the rarebit on top. Cover each with a second slice of toast and spoon remaining rarebit over the toast, dividing it as evenly as possible.

Place the dishes about 2 inches under broiler heat for a few seconds, only until bubbly hot. Serve at once.

Serves 4

NEW ENGLAND RAREBIT

1 cup packaged salt codfish, shredded (or use leftover poached fresh codfish or any other flaked poached fish)
1 tbs. butter
1 tbs. flour
1 tsp. onion, grated
1 cup milk, room temperature (or part milk and part beer or wine)

¾ cup sharp cheddar cheese, grated
1 egg, beaten
4 thick (½ inch) slices from home-style firm, unsliced white bread, lightly toasted

(If using packaged salt codfish follow package directions to freshen.)

Break up fish with a fork.

In a saucepan melt butter and stir in flour. Stir in grated onion, then slowly add milk (or milk and other liquid), stirring as added, and stir until smooth. Add flaked fish and cheese and cook, stirring until sauce thickens.

Beat egg in a small bowl; beat in a little of the hot sauce, then stir into the sauce. Cook, stirring, over low heat a final 4 to 5 minutes.

Spoon over toast and serve at once.

Serves 4 to 6

BAKED FONDUE CASSEROLE

5 eggs separated
1 cup milk
½ lb. natural Swiss cheese cut
    into small cubes (or any
    good natural cheese)
1 tsp. salt

Pinch of dry mustard
Dash Worcestershire sauce
6 slices firm white bread cut
    into small cubes
1 cup beer, or dry white wine
2 tbs. buttered bread crumbs

Preheat oven to 325°F.

In a saucepan beat egg yolks until light, add milk and stir until blended. Add cheese and cook over low heat until cheese melts. Stir in salt, mustard and Worcestershire sauce. Add the bread cubes. Stir to blend and let stand until bread has absorbed sauce. Add beer or wine.

Beat egg whites until stiff and fold into cheese mixture. Turn into well-buttered 1½-quart casserole. Sprinkle surface with buttered bread crumbs. Bake in preheated oven until firm and a knife inserted in center comes out clean. Serve at once.

Serves 6

chapter seven

Pasta

Pasta

Pasta

PASTA—how I love it. Maybe you presently share my enthusiasm for this Italian staple; if not, I am sure you will after you have tried dining Italian style a few times. Inexpensive, delicious and easy, who could ask for more? I like to begin my Italian adventure as they do, with a cold vegetable or two dressed antipasto style with an oil and vinegar dressing, and, perhaps if I'm feeling extravagant, a few black olives.

Here are my favorite antipasto combinations—one for winter, one for summer, both simple and inexpensive yet a perfect beginning to any pasta meal.

WINTER

(asterisk refers to recipe to be found in this book)

JUST BARELY COOKED CARROT "STICKS"
(marinated in the refrigerator until ice cold in
2 tablespoons vinegar mixed with 1
tablespoon sugar and drained well before
serving)

CELERY STALKS
COLD (CANNED) BEETS
ITALIAN OLIVES
VINAIGRETTE DRESSING *

SUMMER

JUST-COOKED GREEN BEANS
(marinated and chilled in the same manner as
the carrots)

JUST-COOKED ZUCCHINI SLICES (AS ABOVE)
WHOLE PLUM TOMATO
UNPEELED CUCUMBER "FINGERS"
ITALIAN OLIVES
VINAIGRETTE DRESSING *

Now add any of the pasta recipes given here, some crusty Italian bread and, of course, a glass or two of red wine.

For dessert, why not finish as the Italians do with a wedge of cheese, a piece of fresh fruit? Tangerines and apples in the winter. Fresh peaches in the summer.

Expresso coffee and perhaps a bowl of nuts (We had tangerines and peanuts at one memorable luncheon in Turino.)

BAKED ZITI WITH BECHAMEL SAUCE

1 1-lb. package ziti #2 (tu-
    bular-shaped pasta)
    (¼ tsp. salt and ½ tsp.
    vegetable oil)
½ cup heavy cream
3 tbs. butter
3 tbs. flour

1½ cup chicken stock, heated
    to boiling (see page 18)
Salt
Pepper
½ cup Parmesan cheese,
    grated

Bring a large pot of water to a full boil. Add salt and oil. Slowly add the ziti so that water continues to boil. Cook 6 to 8 minutes. Drain. Place in a long, shallow baking dish and pour the cream over the surface.

Melt the butter in a saucepan and stir in the flour. Cook, stirring, over low heat for 2 to 3 minutes. Add the boiling stock and stir rapidly with a whisk until smooth. Continue to cook, stirring, until thickened. Season with salt and pepper. Pour over the ziti and cream. Sprinkle with grated Parmesan cheese.

Bake in a preheated 350°F. oven 20 to 25 minutes. Serve from the baking dish.

Serves 6

PASTA WITH SPINACH AND HAM

2 lb. fresh spinach
2 tbs. butter
1 cup leftover baked or
    braised ham, chopped

1 1-lb. package of quadrettini, (small square-shaped pasta) or substitute flat noodles (cooked according to package directions)
Parmesan cheese grated

Wash spinach thoroughly, remove and discard tough stems. Place in a saucepan with only the water clinging to the leaves. Cover and steam only until wilted. Drain and chop.

Melt the butter in a large skillet, add the ham and stir-fry until heated. Stir in the spinach, and the just-cooked drained, still hot quadrettini (or noodles). Sprinkle liberally with grated cheese and serve at once.

Serves 4

QUICK PASTA SAUCES
(All for 4 servings and over 1 lb. cooked pasta)

CHEESE SAUCE
FOR EGG NOODLES

1½ cups cottage cheese   1 1-lb. package fine egg
4 tbs. heavy cream   noodles
4 tbs. Parmesan cheese, grated

Force cottage cheese through a sieve. Stir in cream and grated Parmesan, or place all three ingredients in blender and blend until smooth. Place in a serving bowl large enough to contain both sauce and noodles. Bring to room temperature (put bowl in a pan of hot water for a few minutes). Cook fine egg noodles; drain and immediately add—while still very hot—to sauce in bowl. Mix to blend and serve at once.
Serves 4

ROMAN TUNA SAUCE
FOR FETTUCCINI
OR THIN SPAGHETTI

1 6½-oz. can Italian-style   Salt
  tuna in olive oil   Pepper
½ cup chicken stock (see page   Mixed Italian herbs
  18)   1 1-lb. package thin fettuccini
1 1-lb. can Italian-style stewed   or spaghetti
  tomatoes with basil   Parmesan cheese, grated

Place tuna and tuna oil and stock in electric blender. Blend until smooth. Pour into saucepan, add stewed tomatoes, season lightly with salt, pepper and herbs. Cook, stirring, over very low heat for 15 to 20 minutes or until sauce is thick and smooth. Cook spaghetti; drain and serve immediately with hot tuna sauce poured over.
Pass grated Parmesan cheese to spoon over each serving.
Serves 4

TUNA SAUCE
FOR SPAGHETTI

2 tbs. butter
1 clove garlic, peeled and
    finely minced
1 6½-oz. can Italian-style
    tuna packed in olive oil
½ cup chicken stock (see page
    18)

2 to 3 tbs. parsley, minced
Salt
Pepper
1 1-lb. package spaghetti

Melt butter in a heavy skillet, add garlic and sauté over very low heat until limp. Combine tuna, oil from can and stock in electric blender. Blend until smooth, add to skillet and cook over very low heat for about 10 minutes. Stir in parsley, season to taste with salt and pepper.

Cook spaghetti. Drain and return to hot pot.

Reheat tuna sauce to very hot, add to spaghetti, toss briefly and serve at once.

Serves 4

MARINARA SAUCE
(Meatless Tomato Sauce)
FOR ANY PASTA

2 tbs. salad or olive oil, or
    butter (or 1 tbs. butter, 1
    tbs. oil)
1 large onion, peeled and
    chopped
1 tsp. mixed Italian herbs
8 large ripe tomatoes (about 4
    lbs.)

1 tsp. salt
¼ tsp. coarsely ground black
    pepper
1 6-oz. can tomato paste
2 cups water
⅓ cup sweet vermouth or
    marsala wine

In hot oil in a large, heavy pot, sauté onions, stirring, over low heat until tender, about 10 minutes. Stir in herbs.

Wash tomatoes, remove skins, cut into quarters; add to sautéed onions with salt, pepper, tomato paste and water. Bring to boil, stirring constantly. Reduce heat and simmer partially covered for 45 minutes, stirring occasionally.

Add vermouth or wine, let simmer 15 minutes longer, or until sauce is thick.

Makes about 2 quarts. (sufficient sauce for 3 or 4 pasta meals, using 1-lb. spaghetti or other pasta for each dish)

Notes

For a lighter, very fresh tasting and less expensive sauce, eliminate the tomato paste, water and vermouth or wine. Reduce cooking time by about 15 minutes, and just before serving stir in about ½ cup minced parsley.

For additional flavor in either version, add a few chopped mushroom stems and the chopped onion and proceed as directed; or add about ¼ cup finely minced green, leafy celery tops. They cost nothing if you have fresh mushrooms or celery on hand in the refrigerator saved from another recipe.

RICOTTA SAUCE
FOR GREEN NOODLES

1½ cups ricotta cheese
2 tbs. Parmesan cheese, grated
1 1-lb. package green noodles

4 tbs. butter, room
*   temperature*

Combine ricotta cheese with Parmesan cheese. Bring to room temperature.

Cook noodles; drain. Return them to the hot cooking pot, add butter, and toss quickly. Add cheeses again, toss briefly and serve at once.

Serves 4

TOMATO SAUCE WITH FRESH BASIL
FOR RIGATONI

1 long, thin yellow-red sweet
    pepper
4 large tomatoes
10 to 12 leaves fresh basil,
    torn into shreds
¼ cup olive oil
1 tsp. salt

¼ tsp. coarsely ground black
    pepper
1 8-oz. package mozzarella
    cheese, cubed
1 1-lb. package rigatoni
Parmesan cheese, freshly
    grated

Prepare sauce about 2 hours before serving.

Cut sweet pepper in half, remove seeds and cut into thin strips. Place in a saucepan and cover with cold water. Bring to a boil; let boil 5 minutes. Drain. Blot dry.

Plunge tomatoes into boiling water for a few seconds. Hold under cold water and slip off skins. Cut in half and gently squeeze out seeds. Cut each half into thin slivers.

Combine pepper strips, tomato, basil, oil, salt and pepper in a bowl large enough to contain both sauce and cooked rigatoni, and let stand for about 2 hours at room temperature.

Cook rigatoni according to package directions. Drain and add to vegetable mixture. Add mozzarella cheese cubes and mix quickly but well and serve at once. Pass Parmesan cheese at the table to sprinkle over.

Serves 6

PARSLIED ALFREDO SAUCE
FOR FETTUCCINI

4 tbs. butter
⅓ cup heavy cream
1 1-lb. package flat noodles
    (½ tsp. salt, 1 tbs. oil for
    cooking)

½ cup Parmesan cheese,
    freshly grated
½ cup parsely, finely minced

About 1½ hours before cooking fettuccini, remove butter and cream from refrigerator and let stand in a warm place at room temperature until ready to use. Butter should be very

soft, but not melted. Cream should be almost warm. If necessary, heat cream in a cup in a pan of hot water until sufficiently warm.

Bring a large, heavy pot of water to a full boil. Add salt and
oil; slowly add noodles so that water remains at a boil. Cook
noodles until no starchy flavor remains but they are still a little
firm to the bite—in other words (Italian ones), *al dente.* Drain
them into a colander.

Immediately put the butter into the hot cooking pot and return the noodles to it. Add the cream, the cheese and parsley.
Using 2 forks toss briefly but well and serve at once.

Serves 4 to 6

PEPERONATA SAUCE
(Green Pepper Sauce)
FOR SPAGHETTI

4 large green peppers	*1 tbs. tomato paste*
1 small onion	*¼ cup red wine or water*
1 tbs. butter and 1 tbs. olive	*¼ tsp. mixed Italian herbs*
oil (or all butter; or all oil)	*Salt*
1 1-lb. can tomatoes with basil	*Pepper*
1 cup water or chicken stock	*1 1-lb. package spaghetti*

Place peppers about 3 inches under medium broiler heat.
Roast, turning them frequently (use a long-handled, two-
pronged fork), until they are singed—blistered and black. Remove and slip off the skins. Cut in half, remove seeds and cut
into strips.

Sauté the onion in the butter over low heat until limp, about
10 minutes. Add peppers and continue to cook now over fairly
high heat for about 5 minutes. Add remaining ingredients.
Reduce heat to low and let simmer about 30 minutes or until
sauce is thick and flavors blended. Season with salt and pepper.

Serve over 1 lb. just-cooked and drained very hot spaghetti.

Cook spaghetti. Drain and return to hot pot.

Add sauce, toss briefly and serve at once.

Serves 4

chapter eight

Potatoes, Rice and Beans

STUFFED BAKED POTATOES

The egg, cheese and milk make this recipe qualify as a high protein dish.

4 large baking potatoes
1 tsp. salt
1 pt. cottage cheese, room temperature

1 egg, lightly beaten with ½ cup milk
2 tbs. grated Parmesan cheese

Preheat oven to 400°F.

Scrub the potatoes and pierce each several times with the point of a small, sharp knife. Bake in preheated oven for 1 hour or until done.

Cut potatoes in half, scoop out the insides into a mixing bowl. Add remaining ingredients and first mash, then beat until light and fluffy.

Stuff the potato shells with the mixture and return them to the oven for about 10 minutes.

Serves 4

POTATO CASSEROLE SWISS STYLE

6 medium-size potatoes
Salt
Pepper
4 tbs. butter cut into tiny
    slivers

6 thin slices of Swiss cheese
1 cup clear, fat-free chicken or
    beef stock (see pages 17
    and 18)

Peel and slice the potatoes as thinly as possible. Arrange a layer of potatoes in the bottom of a 2-quart buttered casserole or soufflé dish, sprinkle with salt and pepper, dot with about 1 tbs. of the butter slivers and cover with 3 slices of the cheese. Repeat, then top with a final layer of potatoes. Dot with remaining butter slivers and pour stock over surface. Cover and bake in a preheated 400°F. oven until potatoes are tender. Invert the baking dish on a heated serving dish, turn out and serve at once.

Serves 6

SWEET POTATO SOUFFLÉ

6 medium-size sweet potatoes
2 tbs. brown sugar
¾ cup milk heated with 3 tbs.
    butter

1 tsp. lemon rind, grated
3 egg whites

Boil the potatoes in enough water to cover until tender. Peel while still hot and mash with sugar until smooth. Fold in the hot milk and butter, and continue to beat until light and fluffy. Fold in lemon rind.

Beat the egg whites until stiff but not dry, and fold them into the potato mixture.

Pour into a well buttered 2-quart soufflé dish. Bake in a preheated 375°F. oven until the soufflé is puffed and the top is lightly browned, 30 to 40 minutes. Serve at once.

Serves 6

SCALLOPED TOMATO AND POTATO CASSEROLE

3 medium potatoes (about
   3 lbs.)
3 medium-ripe tomatoes
   (about 2 lbs.)
2 large, mild onions

Seasoned salt
Coarsely ground black pepper
3 tbs. very cold butter cut in
   thin slivers
½ cup fine, dry bread crumbs

Preheat oven to 400°F.

Peel potatoes. Cut potatoes and tomatoes into ¼-inch slices. Peel and slice onion as thinly as possible.

Layer potatoes, then onions, then tomatoes in a shallow casserole dish. Repeat layering ending with tomatoes. Sprinkle each layer with salt and pepper and top each layer of tomatoes with butter slivers, reserving about 1 tbs. butter for later use. Cover dish and bake for 45 minutes or until potatoes are fork tender. Uncover, sprinkle with bread crumbs and dot with reserved butter slivers. Bake uncovered until topping is lightly browned, about 5 minutes.

Serves 6

BAKED GRITS

2 cups just-cooked, still hot
   grits prepared according
   to package directions
2 egg yolks, beaten
½ cup grated American cheese

2 egg whites, beaten until stiff
½ tsp. freshly ground black
   pepper
2 tbs. butter cut into slivers

Preheat oven to 350°F.

Combine hot grits with egg yolks and cheese; blend well. Beat egg whites until stiff, fold into grits, add pepper and pour into a shallow baking dish. Dot with slivers of butter and bake in preheated oven for 25 to 30 minutes or until lightly browned on top.

Serves 6 to 8

CURRIED RICE

You can prepare a meal in minutes by serving this rice dish with cold leftover baked turkey, chicken or ham. Do include the chutney—it really goes with this combination of hot and cold food.

2 tbs. butter	1 tbs. flour
1 small onion, peeled and finely minced	2 cups chicken stock (see page 18)
1 medium-size tart apple, peeled, cored, seeded and finely chopped	½ cup sour cream
	3 cups cooked rice
1 tbs. curry powder	Chutney (see pages 172 and 173)

Melt the butter in a large skillet. In it sauté the onion and apple until onion is limp. Stir in curry powder first, then flour and cook, stirring until smooth. Slowly add the stock, stirring as added. Continue to stir until thick and smooth. Add the sour cream and stir a final 2 to 3 minutes or until sauce is steamy hot. Add the rice and gently fork-stir until it has absorbed the sauce.

Serve very hot accompanied by your own homemade chutney.

Serves 4 to 6

SOY SAUCE RICE
WITH RAISINS AND NUTS

While certainly this rice mixture can be served as part of an Oriental meal, it is equally good as an accompaniment to broiled fish, chicken or meat. Try it with lemon-baked chicken (see page 89). Or serve it with leftover, cold, sliced turkey.

3 cups cooked rice	½ cup pine nuts (or slivered almonds)
¼ cup soy sauce	
½ cup raisins	

Place rice in a greased, shallow baking dish. Sprinkle with soy sauce. Add raisins and pine nuts or almonds. Gently fork-stir to blend. Place in a preheated 350°F. oven and bake, stirring occasionally, for 15 to 20 minutes or until dry.

Serves 4 to 6

RICE CASSEROLE
WITH VEGETABLES AND CHEESE

1 tbs. butter
1 small onion, peeled and
    finely minced
½ small green pepper, all
    white and seeds removed,
    and finely minced
2 cups cooked rice

1 cup chicken stock (see page
    18) or 1 cup milk
2 eggs, lightly beaten
Salt
Coarsely ground black pepper
¼ cup Parmesan cheese,
    grated

Melt butter in a small suacepan over low heat. In it sauté onion and green pepper until limp.

Combine sautéed vegetables, rice, stock and eggs. Fork-stir to blend. Season with salt and pepper. Turn into a buttered 1-quart casserole. Sprinkle with grated cheese. Bake in a preheated 375°F. oven for 30 to 40 minutes or until firm.

Serves 4 to 6

Notes

You can add chopped leftover ham, chicken or turkey to make this a main course dish.

ITALIAN BAKED BEANS

This is a meal in itself with some crusty Italian bread, a glass of wine and a fresh fruit dessert. The fruit depends on the season—just be sure to have plenty of it and sprinkle fairly generously with brandy before serving. (See pages 181–182 for fruit combinations suggestions.)

1 lb. dried red kidney beans
1 onion, peeled and cut in
    quarters
1 clove garlic, peeled and split
1 tbs. butter
2 tbs. onion, minced
1 1-lb. can tomatoes (no need
    to buy whole
    tomatoes—look for a
bargain in stewed
    tomatoes)
½ lb. provolone cheese,
    grated
½ tsp. salt
1 tsp. Italian seasoning
¼ cup dry white wine or
    water

Place beans in a large, heavy oven-proof kettle (enameled cast iron is best), cover with cold water and let soak 6 to 8 hours or overnight. Drain beans, cover with fresh water, add onion quarters and garlic. Bring to a boil, then lower heat and simmer, for about 2 hours or until beans are tender. Drain, remove and discard onion and garlic and set beans aside. Melt butter in a heavy skillet, add minced onion and sauté until limp; add tomatoes and their liquid and cook over low heat until steamy hot, breaking up tomatoes as they cook to form a smooth liquid. Add cheese and stir until melted. Add salt, Italian seasoning and wine. Stir until well blended. Pour over beans in kettle and bake in 300°F. oven for 1 hour.
    Serves 8

A WINTER CHILI BEANS
AND VEGETABLES CASSEROLE

1 1- to 1½-lb. eggplant
Salt
2 tbs. butter
1 tbs. vegetable oil
1 large onion, peeled and
    chopped
1 clove garlic, peeled and
    minced
1 large green pepper, halved,
    seeded and cut into strips
1 1-lb. can stewed tomatoes
2 cups cooked (dried) kidney
    beans; (or 1 15-oz. can
    kidney beans, drained and
    rinsed)
1 tbs. chili powder, (or more if
    needed)

Peel eggplant and cut into 1-inch cubes. Sprinkle generously with salt. Place in a colander and weigh down with a heavy plate. Let stand 30 minutes to drain.

Combine butter and oil in a large, heavy pot. Place over medium heat. When butter has melted, add onion, garlic and green pepper. Cook, stirring, for 5 to 6 minutes. Add tomatoes and beans. Stir in chili powder.

Rinse salt from eggplant cubes and add to mixture, carefully mixing ingredients together. Bring to boiling. Cover, lower heat and let simmer for about 30 minutes.

Serve over just-cooked hot and fluffy white rice.

Pass small bowls of grated American or mild cheddar cheese and shredded lettuce to sprinkle over each serving.

Serves 6 to 8

BOSTON BAKED BEANS

You probably have a recipe for Boston baked beans, but this one is authentic. Besides, whoever heard of a budget cookbook without this classic bean recipe? Serve them some Saturday night with plenty of crisp coleslaw and buttered Boston brown bread. Incidentally, baked beans freeze well, so wrap any leftovers securely and freeze for a repeat performance.

2 lbs. dried pea or great northern beans	1 tsp. salt
1½ cups onion, finely chopped	1 tsp. coarsely ground black pepper
2 tbs. tomato paste	1½ cups brown sugar
2 tbs. vinegar	¼ lb. salt pork, free of rind and cut into small dice
1 tbs. dry mustard	

Wash the beans well by placing in a colander under cold running water. Transfer the beans to a deep, heavy stove-to-oven casserole. Cover with cold water to within 2 inches of rim. Bring to a boil over high heat. Skim off accumulated scum. Boil rapidly for 2 or 3 minutes. Turn off the heat and let beans soak for about 1 hour. Bring the beans back to a boil, lower heat and allow to simmer (over very low heat) for ½ hour.

Drain the beans in a colander over a large bowl. Reserve liquid and return beans to casserole. Pour 2 cups of the liquid into a mixing bowl (reserve remaining liquid) and add all remaining ingredients except ½ cup of the sugar and the salt pork cubes. Blend well and pour over beans in casserole.

Preheat oven to 250°F.

Add pork cubes to casserole, mixing gently to distribute seasonings and pork.

Cover casserole and bake in preheated oven for 4 to 5 hours. Check occasionally; if the beans seem too dry add ½ cup of the reserved bean liquid. When the beans are tender, uncover the pot and spread surface of beans with the remaining brown sugar. Return to the oven and bake uncovered for a final 30 minutes. Serve from the casserole.

Serves 8 to 10

BAKED BEANS TEXAS STYLE

These are hot and spicy, as good as Boston baked beans but quite different in flavor. In the Lone Star State these beans are served with hot corn bread; I like to add a cucumber salad. If you want a really special feast serve them with barbecued hamburgers and maybe a Texas watermelon for dessert.

2 lbs. pea or great northern
   beans
1 6-oz. can tomato paste
3 tsp. chili powder
2 large green chilies (canned),
   finely chopped

3 tsp. dry mustard
2 tbs. brown sugar
¼ cup vinegar
1 tbs. salt
2 tsp. garlic, finely chopped
1 lb. salt pork cut in small dice

Wash the beans and proceed as for Boston beans. When you have completed the parboiling, soaking and simmering, drain the beans as directed reserving cooking liquid. Return beans to casserole.

Preheat oven to 250°F.

Measure 4 cups of the bean liquid into a mixing bowl, reserve any extra liquid. Add all remaining ingredients except pork dice. Beat vigorously with a wire whisk until well blended. Pour over beans. Add salt pork dice and mix gently but thoroughly. Cover casserole tightly and bake for 4 to 5 hours or until beans are tender. Check occasionally; if beans seem dry add ½ cup of the reserved bean liquid. Uncover for the final 30 minutes of cooking to give the beans a crusty finish. Serve from the casserole.

Serves 8 to 10

chapter nine

Vegetables and Salads

VEGETABLES

Given just a little time and a lot of imagination, vegetables can not only pare your food bill, if used in season, but can greatly contribute to the pleasure of the table. And that's what cooking is all about, isn't it?

The vegetable recipes in this book have been divided into seasons because, of course, only in-season vegetables are bargains and only in-season vegetables taste like anything anyway. We begin with zucchini, tomatoes, fresh corn, eggplant and the like.

Many of the recipes here can double as hearty main dishes and no one will feel deprived; as a matter of fact, they offer a welcome change for the better more often than not.

A SUMMER VEGETABLE DINNER
FOR THE TRUE GOURMET

VICHYSOISSE WITH MINCED CHIVES *
ZUCCHINI, TOMATO AND CORN
CASSEROLE *

SAUTÉED EGGPLANT SLICES *
HOT GARLIC BREAD
SWEDISH SHREDDED BEETS
WITH SOUR CREAM *
BLUEBERRY CRUMBLE PIE *

This is heaven on a summer day: serve it outdoors for Sunday lunch under a cloudless sky, or on the terrace just as evening begins—by candlelight of course. Add a chilled white wine or ice cold imported beer.

If this sounds like a lot of different dishes, let me hasten to add that the vichysoisse can be waiting chilled in the refrigerator, the casserole made and refrigerated until time to bake, the eggplant ready for last minute sautéing and the beets prepared and reheated just before serving.

ZUCCHINI, TOMATO
AND CORN CASSEROLE

6 zucchini
3 tbs. butter
1½ cups onion, finely minced
1 clove garlic, finely minced
1 green pepper, cored, seeded
and finely chopped
2 medium tomatoes, peeled
and chopped

½ cup cheddar cheese, grated
3 eggs, well beaten
½ tsp. salt
2 cups fresh kernel corn cut
from the cob
¼ cup fine, dry bread crumbs

Preheat oven to 350°F.

Wash and cut the zucchini into thin rounds, melt the butter in a heavy, deep skillet or saucepan and sauté the zucchini slices until just beginning to become tender. Add the onion, garlic and green pepper and cook over very low heat until vegetables are limp. Add the tomatoes and continue to cook over low heat until tomatoes are liquid. Break tomatoes up with the tip of a spatula as they cook. Remove from heat; add cheese,

eggs, salt and corn. Blend well. Pour into a lightly buttered casserole, sprinkle lightly with bread crumbs and bake in pre-heated oven for 1 hour.
    Serves 6

SAUTÉED EGGPLANT SLICES

1 *large or 2 small eggplant*	2 *tbs. flour*
1 *egg, well beaten*	¼ *tsp. salt*
½ *cup water*	4 *tbs. salad oil*
1 *cup cornmeal*	1 *tbs. butter*

Peel and cut the eggplant into even fairly thick slices. In a shallow dish beat the egg with the water until blended. Blend the cornmeal with the flour and salt in a second shallow dish. Dip each slice, on both sides, into egg-water mixture, then into cornmeal-flour mixture. Place in a shallow pan or on a cookie sheet as each slice is coated with cornmeal. Refrigerate slices for ½ hour or until ready to sauté (up to 3 hours). Heat the salad oil with the butter in a large, heavy skillet and sauté the eggplant slices over medium to low heat for about 3 minutes to each side, turning once to assure even browning. Serve at once or keep hot in a medium 350°F. oven for 15 to 20 minutes before serving.
    Serves 6 to 8

FRESH TOMATO-CUCUMBER SHRUB

A delectable start to a summer-day menu, and easy and cheap too if you wait until tomatoes are in peak season.
    Follow with deviled broiled fish (see page 103), baked grits (see page 140) and broiled peach halves; dessert could be

madeleines (see page 184) and coffee or sponge cake (see page 187) and coffee.

4 large, very ripe summer
    tomatoes
3 or 4 vine-ripened summer
    cucumbers
½ tsp. salt

¼ tsp. coarsely ground black
    pepper
½ tsp. curry powder
3 tbs. mayonnaise

Peel the tomatoes by immersing for a moment or two in boiling water and slipping off the skins with the point of a small sharp knife. Cut into quarters, remove and discard seeds. Place in a mixing bowl and chop very fine with the point of a small sharp knife. Peel cucumbers and mince into fine dice; add salt and pepper. Pour into ice cube trays and freeze to "mushy" stage, stirring occasionally with a wooden spoon to keep crystals from forming. If it gets too hard, don't panic; simply empty into a large bowl and beat lightly with a fork before piling into ice cold soup cups.

Mix curry powder with mayonnaise and top each serving with a spoonful.

Serves 6

FARMHOUSE TOMATOES

This is a lovely luncheon or supper dish. Add canned matchstick potatoes (which are cheap) and finish the meal with a substantial piece of cheese and a piece of fresh fruit.

2 large, firm tomatoes
½ cup flour
1 tsp. salt
½ tsp. coarsely ground black
    pepper
3 tbs. butter

3 tbs. brown sugar
8 slices firm white bread,
    toasted
1 small can potted ham
½ cup cream
2 tbs. parsley, chopped

Wash and cut the tomatoes into thick slices. Combine flour, salt and pepper. Dip tomato slices in flour mixture. Melt the butter in a large, heavy skillet, add the tomato slices in a single layer and sprinkle with half the brown sugar. Cook over low heat so that sugar will melt, turn, sprinkle again with sugar and continue to cook until tomatoes are tender. Keep hot.

Spread toast with potted ham and place on serving plates. Top each piece of toast with a tomato slice.

Add cream to pan in which tomatoes were cooked and heat to bubbling hot, stirring constantly. Pour over tomatoes, sprinkle with parsley and serve at once.

Serves 4

BAKED STUFFED TOMATOES

2 large tomatoes (about 1 lb.)
Salt
2 tbs. butter
1 clove garlic, very finely
    minced
1 cup fine, dry bread crumbs
    (made from hard French
    or Italian bread)

½ tsp. seasoned salt
Coarsely ground black pepper
Corn or safflower oil (or mild,
    fresh olive oil)

Preheat oven to 350°F.

Cut tomatoes in half crosswise. With the handle of a teaspoon carefully scoop the seeds from each half, removing as little of the sectional walls as possible.

Sprinkle the insides of each tomato half with salt and invert on a plate to drain while preparing the stuffing.

In a medium skillet melt the butter. Add the garlic and cook, stirring, over low heat for about 1 minute. Off the heat stir in bread crumbs, seasoned salt and pepper.

Fill each tomato half with this mixture. Arrange them side by side in a large oiled baking dish and dribble a little oil over each.

Bake in preheated oven for 20 to 30 minutes or until soft but not falling apart and the stuffing is lightly browned.

Serves 4

SAUTÉED ZUCCHINI AND
TOMATOES ITALIAN STYLE

1 lb. zucchini	¼ tsp. mixed Italian herbs
1 tbs. butter	¼ tsp. salt
1 small onion, peeled and minced	¼ tsp. coarsely ground black pepper
2 large ripe tomatoes (about 1 lb.)	2 tbs. water
	Parmesan cheese, grated

Wash zucchini well. Slice into ½-inch thick diagonal slices.

In hot butter in a deep, heavy skillet sauté onion until limp, about 2 minutes. Add zucchini slices, tomatoes, herbs, salt, pepper and water. Cover and let steam over low heat 10 to 15 minutes or until zucchini is tender. Sprinkle generously with grated Parmesan cheese and serve at once.

Serves 6

Notes

To serve as a main course;

Brown ½ lb. ground lean beef; add the onion and stir until limp. Add sliced zucchini, tomato and seasonings. Cook as above.

Meal extender:

Serve over 1 lb. flat noodles cooked *al dente* (still slightly firm).

EGGPLANT AND TOMATOES
A LA TURQUE

Here's a very easy and delicious first course to be followed perhaps by Fettuccini Alfredo (pasta with butter, grated Parmesan cheese and lots of parsley). Follow with fresh peaches sprinkled with brown sugar and a little of the red wine you will surely serve for this perfect summer menu. Summer? Of course, for only then are the eggplant, tomatoes, parsley and peaches at their peak of perfection and the bottom of the price scale.

1 large eggplant
1½ tsp. salt
6 ripe tomatoes
4 small purple onions (or three
    large white onions my be
    substituted)

1 tsp. coarsely ground black
    pepper
½ cup mild salad oil
½ cup seasoned bread crumbs
1 tbs. butter

Preheat oven to 250°F.

Peel the eggplant and slice rather thinly, sprinkle with salt and pile the slices on top of one another in a pie plate. Weigh them down with a heavy skillet or any other heavy item to press out juices. (I know one cook who uses her steam iron placed in still another pie plate—precarious but effective). Let slices stand under pressure for 30 minutes. Drain off liquid. Cut larger slices into halves. Peel tomatoes by immersing briefly in boiling water and slipping off skins with the point of a small sharp knife. Slice into fairly thick slices, push out and discard seeds. Peel and slice onions, break slices into rings. Line a 2-quart casserole with a layer of onions, then a layer of eggplant, followed by a layer of tomatoes. Sprinkle with pepper and repeat layers until all vegetables are used, ending with a layer of tomatoes. Pour salad oil evenly over vegetables. Sprinkle with seasoned bread crumbs, dot with slivers of butter and bake in preheated oven for 2½ hours. Serve at room temperature or chilled.

Serves 6

SCALLOPED FRESH CORN CASSEROLE WITH HAM

*8 medium-size ears fresh sweet
    corn (or sufficient to make
    4 cups corn kernels)*
*½ cup lean leftover baked
    ham, chopped*
*¾ cup fine soda cracker
    crumbs*
2 eggs
1½ cups milk
1 tsp. salt

⅛ tsp. pepper
*2 tbs. grated cheese (any
    natural will
    do—Parmesan, cheddar,
    Swiss, brick, etc.)*

Topping
*1 cup fine soda cracker crumbs
    mixed with 4 tbs. melted
    butter*

Cut the kernels from the cob; using a sharp small knife slit down the center of each row of kernels, then scrape all pulp and milk into a bowl.

Layer half the chopped ham and cracker crumbs, then half the corn in a buttered, long, shallow baking dish. Add remaining crumbs, ham and remaining corn.

In a saucepan beat eggs until yolks and whites are mixed. Add milk, blend and add seasoning and cheese. Place over medium heat and stir until cheese is melted and mixture steamy hot. Pour over corn mixture in casserole.

Mix topping cracker crumbs with melted butter and top casserole with mixture.

Place baking dish in a large pan, set on middle oven rack, then pour hot water into pan to come halfway up the baking dish.

Bake in preheated 350°F. oven for about 1 hour or until bubbly hot and topping is lightly browned.

Serves 6

CORN PUDDING

This is a lovely summer dish that makes the most of that most delectable of summer vegetables, fresh corn. Try it for

Sunday lunch with fricassee of chicken. You might begin the menu with cold sliced cucumbers vinaigrette (see page 161) and end it with honeydew or cantaloupe and peach slices sprinkled with a little brandy. Add madeleines (see page 184) and plenty of black coffee in small cups. A bit of brandy in each? Why not?

2 tbs. butter	1¾ cup milk
2 tbs. flour	3 cups fresh corn sliced from
1 tsp. salt	the cob
1 tsp. sugar	3 eggs, lightly beaten

Preheat oven to 350°F.

Melt the butter in a heavy saucepan over very low heat, add flour, blend, and continue to cook for 2 or 3 minutes. Stir in salt and sugar. Slowly add milk and cool until mixture is smooth and begins to thicken. Remove from heat. Add corn, blend; add beaten eggs and blend well. Pour into a lightly buttered casserole. Place casserole in a larger pan of hot water in preheated oven and bake for about 45 minutes.

Serves 6 to 8

SPINACH SOUFFLÉ

3 tbs. butter	2 tbs. natural Swiss or
3 tbs. flour	Parmesan cheese, grated
¼ tsp. salt	Salt
¾ cup chicken stock, heated	Pepper
(see page 18)	
¼ cup milk	
3 eggs, separated	
1 cup fresh spinach, cooked	
thoroughly, drained,	
blotted dry and finely	
chopped	

Preheat oven to 350°F.

Generously butter a 1½-quart soufflé dish.

In a heavy pot melt butter, stir in flour and salt. Cook, stirring, over very low heat for almost 10 minutes. Mixture should be golden in color with a fragrant nutty aroma. Slowly stir in heated stock, then milk; cook, stirring, to a thick smooth sauce.

Beat egg yolks in a large mixing bowl for about 1 minute. Gradually add hot sauce, beating with whisk as it is added. Stir in spinach and grated cheese. Season lightly with salt and pepper.

In a separate bowl beat egg whites until stiff; fold into spinach mixture. Pour into prepared soufflé dish. Place dish in a pan on middle rack of preheated oven and pour hot water in pan to a depth of 1 inch.

Bake soufflé for 45 minutes or until puffed and browned.

Serves 4 to 6

Notes

This tastes great as even spinach haters agree. Serve it with creamed tuna. Add a broiled tomato half to each serving and a gourmet dinner is served.

A WINTER VEGETABLE DINNER

Vegetable dinners are viewed with alarm by most men and a lot of women; it's because vegetable dinners tend to be the low end of the totem pole for most cooks. But all that need not be: vegetable dinners can be sophisticated, hearty fare that will make everyone happy.

One of my favorite centerpieces for a vegetable platter on a cold winter night is cabbage-stuffed cabbage; this is surrounded by glazed whole onions, then glazed sweet potatoes alternating with neat mounds of hot spiced green beans. On the side is a mustard cream sauce for spooning over the cabbage and in a nearby basket are hot corn sticks.

Sounds like a lot of work? Not at all. The cabbage can be prepared ahead and refrigerated until ready to boil. The onions only require peeling, placing in a shallow casserole, dribbled with a bit of butter and about ¼ cup water, then baked (about 1 hour depending on size) until tender and golden. Sweet potatoes are simplicity itself; they are simply boiled for about 20 minutes, peeled and sliced in half. While they cook place ½ cup of brown sugar and 3 tbs. of butter (enough for 4 sweet potatoes or 8 slices) in a shallow baking dish. Place in a slow 250°F. oven until butter melts and sugar begins to liquify. Blend well together, add sweet potato slices and bake at 250°F. for 45 to 50 minutes, basting once or twice to coat with glaze.

Now for the green beans: cook, drain and add 1 tbs. cider vinegar while hot. Serve hot.

For dessert, well, this is a fairly light meal so why not serve slightly warmed slices of applesauce cake, each slice flamed with a teaspoon or so of California brandy? And plenty of hot, strong coffee to go with it, of course.

CABBAGE-STUFFED CABBAGE

The secret here is the cabbage must be fresh, crisp, leafy and green. Look at the stem end: if there is a longish stem indicating a lot of leaves have been pulled off and the cabbage is lacking in green outer leaves, it is not for you. Supermarkets usually try to push not-so-fresh vegetables and if the cabbage in the bin is a pallid white (too many people think this is the way cabbage "just is"), pass it up and ask if they have any fresh cabbage they haven't put out yet. They usually do and if you are politely insistent you can probably get them to bring it out. Otherwise buy your cabbage at the more expensive service-type grocery where they specialize in fresh produce, or best yet, from a farm stand where maybe the cabbage is the just-picked variety. It's worth the extra few pennies, for cabbage is cheap.

1 medium to large fresh green
   cabbage
4 tbs. butter
1 medium onion, peeled and
   minced
½ cup bread crumbs
   (homemade in a blender
   from stale bread or rolls)

2 eggs, lightly beaten
1 tsp. Spice Parisienne
¼ tsp. salt
¼ tsp. coarsely ground black
   Java pepper

Tear off any broken or badly soiled outer leaves of the cabbage and discard. Now carefully remove 5 whole outer leaves. Line a good-size mixing bowl with a large square of cheese cloth, leaving the edges hanging over the sides. Arrange the cabbage leaves in the bowl, overlapping and stem ends up to form a large cup closed at the bottom. Set aside while you prepare filling.

Chop remaining cabbage very finely, discarding tough stems and center core. Melt the butter in a heavy skillet and sauté the cabbage in it over low heat until cabbage is soft and golden. Add minced onion and sauté until onion is limp. Add bread crumbs, beaten eggs and seasonings; mix well to blend. Pour mixture into prepared cabbage cup. Pull ends of cheese cloth up and tie securely to form a tight ball. Bring a large kettle of water to a full rolling boil and lower cabbage into it. Immediately reduce heat to simmer and cook, barely simmering, for 1 hour. Remove from water, drain in colander and unwrap. Keep hot in colander over simmering water until ready to serve.

To serve cut in 6 wedges with a sharp knife.

Serves 6

TURNIPS

I find it simply amazing that a lot of people have never eaten turnips. Properly prepared they are a great delicacy, and if anyone should present you with a gift of wild game, turnips are the classic accompaniment. They're equally good with any kind of broiled or roasted fowl or meat.

8 to 12 small white turnips
½ tsp. salt
1 tsp. sugar
1 tbs. cream

¼ tsp. coarsely ground black
pepper

Peel and cut turnips into small dice. Place in a heavy saucepan and add just enough cold water to cover; add salt and sugar and bring to a boil. Lower heat to simmer and continue to cook until turnips are very soft and water has almost evaporated. If the turnips are done but there is too much water, turn heat to high and boil off. Using a wooden spoon, mash the turnips until smooth. Stir in pepper and cream when ready to serve. Reheat briefly to steamy hot, stirring constantly to prevent burning, and serve at once.

Serves 6

PARISIENNE CARROTS
AND ONIONS

Carrots and onions suffer from being plentiful and too cheap. No doubt, if they were rare, hard to get and expensive people would cook them with the care and imagination they deserve and everyone would clamor for carrots. Close your eyes to how little they cost and try this recipe from Paris where the thrifty French know how to make a *specialité* out out of low-cost ingredients.

¼ cup salad oil
2 medium onions, peeled and
    cut in quarters
1½ lbs. carrots, scraped,
    washed and cut into
    2-inch pieces
    (if the carrots are large,
    halve each piece and cut
    out woody centers)
½ cup water

2 cloves garlic, very finely
    minced
½ tsp. Spice Parisienne
½ tsp. pepper
½ tbs. butter
1 tbs. flour
¼ cup beef stock (see page 17)
¾ cup sherry wine (or dry red
    wine plus 1 tsp. sugar)

Heat the salad oil in a deep, heavy saucepan, add the onions and sauté over very low heat until limp. Add the carrots, water, and garlic; cover and steam 10 to 15 minutes, stirring occasionally, until carrots are almost tender. Add seasoning and blend. Remove from heat.

In a small skillet melt the butter; add the flour and cook over low heat, stirring constantly to blend, for 2 or 3 minutes. Slowly add the beef stock and stir to blend until thick and smooth. Add to carrots in saucepan; add wine. Blend well and cook over low heat until steamy hot. Serve as an accompaniment to Meat Loaf (see page 56), add crusty French bread, a glass of dry red wine, and conclude the feast with winter fruit compote topped with a little sour cream.

Serves 4 to 6

SWEDISH SHREDDED BEETS
WITH SOUR CREAM

Use canned or fresh beets—which ever are less expensive. I hope it's the fresh variety, though you must cook them first (see easy way below). They definitely make for a superior tasting dish.

1 tbs. butter
1 small white onion, peeled
    and minced
4 cups cooked or canned beets
    cut in julienne strips
    (If using canned beets, drain
    thoroughly and blot dry.)

½ tsp. dry mustard
½ tsp. salt
Pinch of pepper
½ cup sour cream, room
    temperature
1 tbs. bottled horseradish

Melt the butter in a large, heavy skillet over medium heat. Add the onion and sauté until limp. Mix in beets. Cook until heated.

Mix together remaining ingredients and add to skillet. Cook, stirring gently, until heated—do not allow to boil.

Serves 4 to 6

SALADS

A salad can be all good things to all good cooks: a light touch to a heavy main course, a bright beginning to luncheon or dinner, an accompaniment, like fresh fruit salad with slices of turkey, or a meal in itself. Some of the best warm-weather meals feature salads as the star attraction. In this collection I have avoided the expensive greenery and concentrated on bargain salad fare to make the most of a meal and the least dent in the budget.

COLD SLICED CUCUMBERS VINAIGRETTE

The kind of cucumbers you want for this are the small fresh crisp garden variety. As a matter of fact, if you have any garden at all why not grow a few cucumbers? They are the easiest of vegetables to grow. At any event, once you have acquired the cucumbers here is a delicious and easy way to serve them.

8 to 10 small cucumbers	*1 tbs. fresh chives or young*
1 tsp. salt	*green onions, finely*
¼ cup oil	*minced*
2 tbs. apple cider vinegar	*1 tsp. parsley, finely minced*
2 tsp. sugar	

Wash the cucumbers but do not peel; with a sharp knife slice them as finely as possible (this is easy if you use a chopping board). Place in a thin layer in a shallow glass dish and sprinkle with salt. Allow to stand for about 1 hour at room temperature.

Mix oil, vinegar, and sugar together and beat until sugar is dissolved. Pour over cucumbers, sprinkle with chives or minced green onions and parsley. Refrigerate for at least 3 hours before serving.

Serve with lightly buttered rounds of French bread.

Serves 6

TEXAS TOMATO SALAD

Fresh homegrown tomatoes or the next thing to them, vine-ripened tomatoes from a local farmer, taste superb when prepared in this way and served at room temperature.

4 large tomatoes (about 2 lbs.)	*1 tbs. cider vinegar*
2 tbs. sugar	*2 tbs. mild salad oil*
1 tsp. salt	*3 to 4 dashes tabasco sauce*
⅛ tsp. coarsely ground black	*Green onion tops, minced*
pepper	

Wash tomatoes, blot dry and cut into ¼-inch thick slices. Arrange slightly overlapping on a long, shallow serving dish or deep platter.

Combine remaining ingredients, except green onion tops, and beat with a whisk until sugar has dissolved. Pour over tomato slices, sprinkle with green onion tops. Cover and let stand at room temperature for about 1 hour before serving. Serve at room temperature.

Serves 4 to 6

JELLIED GAZPACHO SALAD

This is my own adaptation of the famous Spanish soup. It makes a festive beginning for dinner, or served with a grilled deviled ham sandwich it's a pleasant midsummer lunch.

2 envelopes unflavored gelatin
3 cups tomato juice
1 clove garlic, peeled
½ cup cucumber, finely diced
¼ cup green onions, minced
    (white part only)

¼ cup celery, finely minced
1 tbs. mayonnaise
1 tbs. sour cream

Soak gelatin in a small amount of cold water to soften. Bring tomato juice to a boil over medium heat. Add garlic clove, pour over softened gelatin and stir until gelatin dissolves. Remove and discard garlic. Refrigerate until thick but not set.

Mix minced vegetables together and fold equally into thickened tomato aspic. Pour into 6 individual molds that have been lightly greased with mayonaise or salad oil. Chill until firm. Unmold onto salad plates and garnish with a spoonful of mayonnaise and sour cream blended together.

Serves 6

SPINACH SALAD
WITH PORK BITS

A long-time favorite of mine and wonderfully good, try it as an accompaniment to beef and kidney pie as one famous New York restaurant does. Need I add that spinach and salt pork are cheap?

1 large purple onion, peeled,
*   sliced and the slices*
*   broken into rings*
½ cup milk
¼ lb. salt pork cut into
*   ½-inch dice*

1 lb. fresh, crisp spinach
2 tbs. vinegar
1 tbs. sugar

Place the onion rings in a shallow nonmetal dish, pour milk over rings and allow to stand at least 1 hour before using. Place salt pork in a small frying pan and cook over low heat until crisp and all fat has been rendered. Remove dice, drain on absorbent paper and set aside. Reserve rendered fat. Keep liquid at room temperature.

Wash spinach thoroughly by filling kitchen sink with cold water and immersing spinach in it. Swish around until all vestiges of sand are removed; repeat if necessary. Tear spinach into bite-size pieces, discarding tough stems and center cores. If you have more spinach than needed, wrap in a damp tea cloth and store in refrigerator. It will stay fresh and crisp up to a week. Keep towel moist.

Pour rendered fat from salt pork into a salad bowl, add vinegar and sugar and blend until sugar has dissolved. Drain onion rings on absorbent paper and add along with spinach to the bowl. Toss well, sprinkle crisp pork bits over surface and serve at once.

Serves 6 to 8

GREEN NOODLE SALAD

This makes a hearty one-dish luncheon or supper with the addition of a little leftover cold roast beef, ham, turkey or chicken. Served without meat it can accompany cold sliced meat or a variety of delicatessen cold cuts for an equally satisfying meal.

2 lbs. flat green noodles	1 tbs. celery seed
½ tsp. salt	½ tsp. salt
2 tsp. salad oil	1 tsp. coarsely ground black
½ cup celery, diced	pepper
½ cup sweet pickles, diced	1 cup mayonnaise
¼ cup parsley, minced	

Bring a large pot of water to a full rolling boil, add salt and salad oil. Add noodles a little at a time to keep water boiling, stir quickly, reduce heat slightly, cook until tender but still slightly firm (al dente). Drain into a colander and rinse immediately with cold water to stop cooking. Place in large salad bowl and add all ingredients except dressing. Toss to blend. Allow salad to cool slightly before adding dressing. Blend well and refrigerate until ready to serve.

Serves 8 to 10

MACARONI SALAD

1 1-lb. package elbow macaroni cooked according to package directions, drained, rinsed and chilled.	¼ cup olives, finely minced (optional)
	1 cup mayonnaise
	½ tsp. curry powder
	1 tbs. lemon juice
1 cup celery, finely minced	
½ cup sweet pickles, finely minced	
1 tsp. onion juice	
¼ cup parsley, finely minced	

Place well-drained, chilled macaroni in a mixing bowl. Add all remaining ingredients, except mayonnaise, curry powder and lemon juice. Toss to blend well. Combine mayonnaise, curry powder and lemon juice. Beat with a whisk to blend. Pour over salad and mix well with a fork to distribute dressing. Cover and refrigerate 2 to 3 hours to mellow flavors. Serve cold.

Serves 8 to 10

Notes

Always keep salads with mayonnaise ice cold so they won't spoil.

BEET AND ORANGE SALAD

This is a special, easy and good inexpensive winter salad.

1 1-lb. can sliced beets, drained	*1 tsp. sugar*
½ cup vinegar	*½ tsp. salt*
	2 large navel oranges

Place beets in a large nonmetal bowl. Combine vinegar, sugar and salt and pour over beets. Marinate for several hours, turning occasionally. Cut oranges into 4 thick slices. With kitchen shears cut off rind and white pith. Drain beets thoroughly and arrange on salad plates with orange slices. Sprinkle with Piquant dressing before serving (see page 167).

Serves 4

ORANGE AND ONION SALAD

2 large purple onions, peeled, sliced and broken into rings	*2 large naval oranges*
½ cup milk	*Piquant dressing (recipe follows)*

Place onion rings in a shallow nonmetal dish so that rings are evenly covered with milk. Allow onions to soak in milk for several hours or overnight. Remove from milk and drain well on paper toweling.

Cut each orange into 4 even slices; with kitchen shears cut away skin and white pith. Arrange orange slices and onion rings on salad plates. Cover with about 1 tbs. of Piquant dressing. Chill until ready to serve.

Serves 4

PIQUANT DRESSING

¼ cup peanut or other salad *oil*
1 tbs. vinegar
1 tsp. sugar

Two or three drops of tabasco sauce
Dash of cayenne pepper

Beat well with a fork until ingredients are well blended and sugar has dissolved.

Serves 4

APPLE AND CABBAGE COLESLAW

I love coleslaw, perhaps because I was determined to make it taste great. It's lovely and cheap and so easy. What's more, cabbage is marvelous for you, a rich source of vitamins A and C. And it tastes so great when it's properly made. If you don't like coleslaw, try this recipe—it's guaranteed to change your mind. And if you want to serve a superb cheap meal, try corn-meal loaf with giblet gravy (see page 97), coleslaw and cold beer. Wind up with apple betty (see page 200) and good coffee.

1 medium head fresh, crisp,
    green cabbage
1 tbs. salt
1 tart crisp apple
1 tsp. onion juice (obtained by

scraping a cut onion with
    a small knife)
2 tbs. fresh lemon juice
1 tbs. sugar
4 tbs. mayonnaise

The secret to good coleslaw is chopping. You'll need a chopping board and a good sharp knife; I use a cleaver.

Tear any wilted, bruised leaves from the cabbage; there won't be many if you have picked your cabbage with care. Cut it into quarters and place in a large pan or bowl of cold water, add the salt and let the cabbage stand in the cold salted water for 10 to 15 minutes. Drain and wash under cold running water. Place cabbage on the chopping board and cut off the white core. Shred as finely as possible. Now peel, core and quarter the apple. Add to the shredded cabbage and start chopping. Chop until every scrap of apple and cabbage is chopped fine, fine, fine. If this sounds like a lot of work, it isn't and it's the only way to make superb coleslaw.

Mix the onion juice, lemon juice, sugar and mayonnaise together in a large bowl and blend until sugar is dissolved. Add the chopped apple and cabbage and blend well. Cover the bowl and refrigerate at least 2 to 3 hours before serving to allow flavors to mellow.

Serves 6

Notes

If there is any leftover (there never is at my house), cover and refrigerate. It tastes even better the next day.

CORN SALAD

1 can whole kernel-style corn
½ green pepper, finely
    chopped and white
    membrane removed
1 cup celery, finely minced
2 tbs. parsley, finely minced

1 tbs. onion, grated
3 tbs. mayonnaise
Juice of ½ lemon
½ tsp. sugar
2 or 3 drops of Tabasco sauce
Cayenne pepper

Combine all ingredients in a large salad bowl and mix well. Sprinkle with cayenne pepper and chill at least 3 hours to allow flavors to mellow before serving.

Serves 4 to 6

FRENCH POTATO SALAD

Potato salad is one of the most useful of salads, especially so for the budget-minded cook. It can be combined successfully with almost any meat or vegetable, and is equally at home on a buffet table or at a country picnic. It's hearty, filling and, prepared in the French manner, really delicious.

¼ cup cider vinegar
1 tsp. dry mustard
2 tsp. salt
2 to 3 dashes hot pepper sauce
  (see page 179)
8 medium-size California
  white potatoes

¾ cup mild salad oil
3 tbs. green onions, finely
  minced
3 tbs. parsley, finely minced

In a large mixing bowl beat vinegar with mustard, salt and pepper sauce until blended. Let stand at room temperature while boiling potatoes.

Boil potatoes in water to cover until done—but not over done; they should be easy to pierce with a two-pronged fork, but not so soft that they will break apart when touched.

Drain, peel and cut each potato while still hot. Place the cubes in the bowl with vinegar mixture and toss them gently (so they don't break up) to coat them with the mixture.

(To peel hot potatoes hold with a long kitchen fork under cold running water and very quickly pull off skin with a small sharp knife—the potato will stay hot but you won't burn your fingers.)

When all the potatoes are peeled, cubed and tossed with the vinegar mixture, slowly add the oil, gently turning the potatoes with a spatula as it is added until each cube glistens with oil. Add the minced green onion and parsley and gently toss to blend. Taste and add salt as needed.

Cover salad and let stand at room temperature 1 hour, or several, until ready to serve.

It may be stored in the refrigerator until time to serve if necessary, but do bring to room temperature before serving. It tastes ever so much better than if chilled.

Serves 6 to 8

VINAIGRETTE DRESSING

Purists may scream at this recipe—sugar, they say, has no place in a salad dressing. I say, just don't say anything. No one will know that the sugar is the reason they suddenly like salads.

1 cup salad oil
¼ cup cider vinegar
1 tbs. sugar

¼ tsp. salt
¼ tsp. coarsely ground black pepper

Combine all ingredients in a mixing bowl and beat with a wire whisk until well blended and sugar is dissolved. Or pour everything into a mason jar and shake vigorously. Store in the jar in the refrigerator.

Great on sliced tomatoes, cold cooked green beans or broccoli, sliced cucumbers and, of course, salad greens.

POPPY SEED DRESSING

½ cup sugar
½ tsp. dry mustard
¼ tsp. salt
¼ cup vinegar

*¼ tbs. onion juice ***
¾ cup salad oil (not olive oil)
1 tbs. poppy seeds

Combine sugar, mustard, salt, vinegar and onion juice. Mix thoroughly. Add oil very slowly, beating as it is added. Naturally this is easier with an electric blender or an electric mixer. Add poppy seeds and beat a few seconds longer. It should be quite thick. Store in the refrigerator; if dressing separates beat for a few minutes before serving.

Makes about 1 cup dressing.

Note

Onion juice is obtained by grating a small onion on the fine side of a hand grater.

chapter ten

Jams, Jellies, Preserves and Pickles

MANGO CHUTNEY

*3 large mangos, peeled, seeded
    and chopped into about 1-
    inch cubes*
3 cups light brown sugar
3 cups apple cider vinegar
2 cups seedless raisins
*½ cup ginger root, cut into
    ¼-inch cubes*
1 cup chopped onion

*2 cloves garlic, peeled and
    minced*
*1 fresh chili pepper, seeded
    and chopped (or 2 tsps.
    red hot pepper flakes)*
*1 tsp. dry mustard mixed to a
    paste with 2 tbs. water*
*1 2-inch stick cinnamon
    broken up*

Combine ingredients in a large 5- to 6-quart heavy pot. Bring to a boil, lower heat and let simmer for about 1 hour, stirring frequently. Remove from heat. Let cool and stand overnight. Reheat to boiling, lower heat and again let simmer for about 1 hour. Let cool, stirring occasionally.

Ladle into clean jars and seal.

Makes about 4 half-pint jars.

RED-HOT TOMATO CHUTNEY

This is more like a dipping sauce than a chutney. It's smooth, not chunky like the Major Gray variety, with a marvelous deep, rich flavor. A perfect accompaniment to an authentic curry dish. Try it too with scrambled eggs as a light supper dish. Caution: use sparingly. It's hot, hot, hot.

3 lbs. ripe tomatoes
1 fresh red chili pepper
1 lb. raisins
2 cloves garlic, peeled
1 pt. cider vinegar

4 cups sugar
¼ lb. green ginger, peeled and
*   chopped*
2 tbs. salt

Place tomatoes in a large pot and pour boiling water to cover over them. Remove each with a long-handled fork, hold under cold water and slip off skins. Slice each into a second pot.

Cut chili pepper in half lengthwise, remove and discard seeds. Chop coarsely.

Place raisins, garlic, chili pepper and ¼ cup vinegar in electric blender. Blend until smooth. Pour over tomatoes; add remaining vinegar, sugar, ginger and salt. Blend and simmer over low heat for about 2 hours, stirring occasionally, or until smooth and thick. Ladle into 4 1-quart jars and seal.

Notes

You don't like it hot? Just leave out the chili pepper. Don't, however, eliminate the garlic—it adds great flavor. And, if you didn't know, the fresh ginger cancels out the garlic "fragrance" and makes it a mild seasoning.

TOMATO MARMALADE

1 lemon
1 thick-skinned, seedless
*   orange*
3 lbs. ripe tomatoes (about 6
*   large ones)*

½ tsp. ground ginger
2 lbs. sugar

Sterilize 6 half-pint jars (see note below).

Pell lemon and orange. Chop peelings. Reserve peeled fruit. Place chopped peels in a saucepan and cover with water. Let simmer over low heat for about 1 hour. Drain.

Plunge each tomato into boiling water for about half a minute. Use a long-handled fork, hold under cold running water, and with the aid of a small sharp knife slip off skins. Chop coarsely. Place in a large, heavy pot. Chop and add peeled fruit, chopped fruit peelings and ginger. Bring to boiling, reduce heat and simmer uncovered for 1 hour. Add sugar; boil uncovered, stirring frequently, until thick, 25 to 30 minutes.

Ladle into hot jars. Immediately cover with ⅛-inch hot paraffin.

Makes 6 half-pint jars

Notes

To sterilize jars and lids, wash in hot soapy water, rinse thoroughly. Place on rack in a large kettle. Add water to cover. Bring water to boiling. Reduce heat, simmer 10 minutes. Leave in hot water. When ready to fill remove from water with tongs.

To Melt Paraffin

Use a container with a pouring spout to melt the paraffin and one you can devote exclusively to this use. Look for those small coffee pots minus their inner workings which thrift shops always seem to have. Place it on an asbestos pad or in a pan of water over low, low heat, until the paraffin is melted. Keep warm or remelt when ready to use.

GREEN PEPPER JELLY

8 to 10 fresh chili peppers
1½ cups cider vinegar
6 cups sugar

1 bottle Certo
3 drops green food coloring

Wash peppers. Cut in half lengthwise and scrape out seeds. Place in a glass jar and pour vinegar over them. Cover and refrigerate for a week to 10 days. Strain, pour into a large, heavy saucepan and add sugar. Stir over low heat until sugar dissolves. Bring to a full boil. Remove from heat and stir in Certo; cook, stirring, until mixture again comes to a boil. Remove from heat and let stand 5 minutes. Stir in food coloring. Pour into clean jars and seal.

Makes about 5½-pint jars.

BRANDIED PEACHES

6 lbs. large clingstone peaches   1½ pts. water
6 lbs sugar   3 pts. brandy

Pour boiling water over peaches. Remove from hot water one by one using a long-handled fork. Hold under cold running water and slip off skins.

In a large, heavy pot boil sugar with water until clear. Add fruit a few pieces at a time and boil until tender but not soft. They must remain whole. Place fruit on a large platter as boiled. Repeat until all fruit has been cooked. Let syrup boil until thick. Cool, add brandy and stir well. Place fruit in sterilized jars. Cover with the syrup to overflowing. Seal.

PICKLED PEACHES

Follow above recipe for brandied peaches, adding 2 tbs. stick cinnamon and 2 tbs. whole cloves. Substitute a good quality cider vinegar for the brandy.

WATERMELON RIND PRESERVES

Rind from 1 large not-too-ripe   *Sugar*
watermelon   *6 to 8 whole cloves*
Rind from 3 squeezed lemons   *1 2-inch stick cinnamon,*
with some remaining pulp   *crumbled*

Peel and discard green watermelon rind. Cut the white pulp into small cubes of approximately the same size.

Cut lemon rind into thinnest possible strips; then cut strips into 1-inch lengths.

Measure watermelon rind and place in a very large nonmetal bowl (or use two bowls—rinds should fill bowl no more than half full). Place lemon peels over surface. For every 4 cups of melon rind use 3 cups of sugar. Dump sugar over surface of melon and lemon rind. Don't stir. Refrigerate overnight. Sugar will melt and liquify.

Dump contents of bowl in a large preserving pot; add cloves and cinnamon. Place over medium heat and bring to a boil. Lower heat and let simmer for about 2 hours. Ladle into sterilized jars and seal. Store in a dark, dry and slightly cool place for about 1 month before using.

BREAD-AND-BUTTER PICKLES

These pickles are crisp and mildly sweet but also a bit tart. Served with slices of French bread spread with soft sweet butter, they make for a truly satisfying luncheon sandwich.

They are quick and easy to make, and, if you prepare them at the height of the cucumber season, they will cost about a quarter the price of the commercial variety.

20 *pickling cucumbers*
  approximately 4 inches
  long
  (Or if not available use
  small cucumbers. Do not
  use cucumbers that have
  been waxed.)
3 ½ *cups sugar*

2 ½ *cups cider vinegar*
1 *cup water*
1 *tbs. salt*
1 *tbs. celery seed*
1 *tbs. white mustard seed*
1 *tbs. mixed pickling spices*
  (wrapped in cheese cloth
  and tied securely)

Wash cucumbers, trim off ends and scrape off any dark spots or marks. Place in a large preserving kettle, and add remaining ingredients. Bring to a full boil, then lower heat and let simmer for 10 minutes. Remove and discard pickling spices.

Ladle cucumbers into freshly washed, rinsed and well-drained jars and cover them with the syrup. Use a slotted spoon to fish the heavy seeds from the bottom of the pot and divide them equally among the jars. Seal the jars and turn them upside down to cool.

Makes about 5 pints

DILLED GREEN BEANS

4 *lbs. whole green beans*
1 ½ *tsps. cayenne pepper*
8 *cloves garlic*
8 *dill heads (or 2 tbs. dill seed)*

4 *cups vinegar*
4 *cups water*
6 *tbs. salt*

Wash beans; cut off ends. Pack lengthwise in clean, hot, pint jars, leaving ¼ inch of headroom. Add 1 clove of garlic, 1 head of dill (or 1 tsp. dill seed) and ¼ tsp. cayenne pepper to each pint jar. Mix together in a enameled kettle the water, vinegar and salt; bring to a boil and pour, boiling hot, over the beans in the jars. Leave ¼ inch headroom. Adjust the lids and process in a boiling water bath (212°F.) for 10 minutes.

Let stand about 2 weeks before serving.

Makes about 6 to 8 pints

HOMEMADE MUSTARDS AND CONDIMENTS

MUSTARD

4 ozs. powdered mustard
¼ cup sugar
1 tbs. salt
½ cup cider vinegar

4 tbs. mild salad oil
2 to 3 dashes tabasco sauce
1 tsp. Worchestershire sauce

Blend mustard, sugar and salt. Add remaining ingredients. Blend to a smooth paste.

This is hot. For a milder mustard blend mixture with equal parts of mayonnaise.

FRENCH WINE MUSTARD

This is similar to the very expensive imported Dijon variety.

4 ozs. dry mustard
⅛ tsp. salt
4 cloves

1 tbs. onion juice
1 cup dry white wine

Blend mustard, salt and cloves. Add remaining ingredients. Blend to a smooth paste.

HOMEMADE MUSTARD

Buy a large can of dry mustard.
Mix as needed:
1 tbs. dry mustard   4 to 6 tbs. water

Blend just before using.
or

For sharper taste use part water, part cider vinegar.
or
For a more subtle, sophisticated flavor use part water, part dry white wine.
or
Mix dry mustard into mayonnaise to taste.

HOT PEPPER SAUCE

2 small, fresh chili peppers   *Olive oil to cover*
1 tbs. vinegar

Use kitchen shears to cut peppers as finely as possible into a small earthenware or glass pot (like a mustard pot), add vinegar and cover with about 2 inches of olive oil.

Use instead of commercially made hot pepper sauce.

This will keep several weeks in the refrigerator. If left too long at room temperature the oil becomes rancid.

ITALIAN GARLIC SAUCE

2 large ripe tomatoes   *1 or 2 fresh basil leaves*
2 cloves garlic, peeled and   *(optional)*
minced   *Olive oil*

Plunge tomatoes into boiling water. Hold under cold water and slip off skins. Cut each in half and squeeze out seeds. Cut each half into small pieces over a small skillet to retain all juice. Place over low heat; add garlic, basil leaves and about 1 tbs. olive oil. Let simmer, chopping the tomato with the tip of a spatula as it cooks until reduced to a pulp. Transfer to a small earthenware or glass jar and cover with an inch or two of olive oil. Cover and refrigerate. This will keep for 1 to 2 weeks. Use to season tomato or any other sauce for pasta, chicken, seafood or meat.

TARRAGON VINEGAR

Fill wide-mouth jar with leaves and stalks of fresh tarragon. Cover with cider vinegar. Let stand 2 to 3 weeks (in the sun when possible). Strain. Use in preparing French dressing, mayonnaise or any sharp sauce.

DILL VINEGAR

Substitute fresh dill for tarragon. Prepare as above.

IDELLE'S MUSTARD SAUCE

Idelle Wright presides over the kitchen at the Women's Exchange here in Pinehurst, North Carolina, and I first tasted this sauce spread on her superb home-baked ham sandwiches. It is heaven on ham, but I like it on cold beef or lamb, and just try it on hamburgers. It's easy and cheap too—what more could you ask?

¼ cup sugar	1 tsp. salt
¾ cup milk	Milk
3 tbs. flour	1 egg yolk, beaten slightly
2 tbs. dry mustard	½ cup white vinegar, warm

Heat the sugar and milk in the top of a double boiler until sugar melts.

In another pan mix the flour, mustard, salt and enough milk to make a paste. Then add the egg yolk and blend. Add paste mixture to milk and sugar in double boiler, stirring to blend. When mixture begins to thicken, add the warm vinegar, stirring until smooth.

chapter eleven

A Collection of Desserts

Desserts add the final fillip to a meal, and, especially if you are really sticking to a strict budget, desserts can actually help to bring the cost of good eating down. For example, a low-cost, delicious and high protein vegetable dinner can end on a festive note with a good dessert, such as applesauce cake laced with brandy or a good pie (my favorites are given here). Main dish soups can be rounded out with a deep-dish fruit pie, and my favorite desserts, fresh fruits, can not only end the meal with a flourish, they can balance it nutritionally as well. For example, a hearty casserole of baked beans, accompanied by a glass of wine and some crusty bread can be balanced by a dessert of seasonal fresh fruit, always a good buy, without feeling guilty that the expensive mixed green salad is skipped. But the real point is that fresh seasonal fruit is not only a bargain both in price and nutrition but can, with a little imagination, be the most delicious ending any meal ever had. Add a basket of madeleines or "Anything Goes" cookies for hearty eaters, or, for the rest of us, any of the following:

SUMMER

ASSORTED MELON SLICES—
CANTALOUPE, WATERMELON, HONEYDEW
(Whatever is in season, available and a good buy)
SPRINKLED WITH FRESH MINT AND POWDERED SUGAR

FRESH PEACH SLICES
WITH BLUEBERRIES
SPRINKLED WITH BRANDY
AND CONFECTIONERS SUGAR

FRESH PEACH HALVES
BAKED IN RED WINE AND A LITTLE SUGAR
TOPPED WITH SOUR CREAM

FRESH STRAWBERRIES
WASHED AND HULLED
SERVED AT ROOM TEMPERATURE
WITH BROWN SUGAR AND SOUR CREAM

WASHED AND HULLED FRESH STRAWBERRIES
SPRINKLED WITH A LITTLE SUGAR AND BRANDY AND
ALLOWED TO STAND AT ROOM TEMPERATURE
FOR AT LEAST ONE HOUR
SERVED OVER SPONGE CAKE
OR
WITH A LITTLE SOUR CREAM

ANYTHING GOES COMPOTE:
WATERMELON AND OTHER MELON BALLS,
PEACH SLICES, BLUEBERRIES, STRAWBERRIES
(Whatever is a bargain at the moment)
MARINATED IN A LITTLE BRANDY WITH A SPRINKLING OF SUGAR

WINTER

ORANGE SLICES
WITH BROWN SUGAR AND SOUR CREAM

BROILED GRAPEFRUIT
CUT FROM THE SHELL AND CORED FOR EASY EATING
SPREAD WITH BUTTER AND BROWN SUGAR BEFORE BROILING

BANANAS FLAMBÉ

Bananas split in half lengthwise, placed in a heavy skillet or chafing dish, the juice of one orange and a tablespoon each of white or brown sugar and brandy added for each banana. Heat until almost all orange juice has evaporated, sprinkle again with brandy, ignite, and bring flaming to the table.

BUDGET BAKED BANANAS

Bananas split lengthwise, spread with homemade marmalade, dotted with butter and baked until soft and golden (about ten minutes) served with sour cream.

MY FAVORITE AMBROSIA
(8 servings)

Three grapefruit cut into sections; six oranges, quartered, then cut from their peel (easy and no white membrane to add bitterness); 1 small can unsweetened pineapple, cut into small pieces; one small can coconut. Mix it all up and let stand in refrigerator at least three hours before serving. Absolutely gorgeous and festive enough for a party.

COOKIES

Buying cookies ranks as a cardinal sin to the disciple of eating well for less money.

Here are two recipes I like that are really all you need. The first one, delicate buttery French madeleines made famous by Proust, is absolutely perfect as an elegant accompaniment to tea or coffee and lovely to serve with a fruit or frozen dessert for even the most special dinner party. Madeleines keep well if they are packed in an air-tight container and stored in the refrigerator.

The second is for what I call, "Anything Goes" Cookies. I add anything on hand; one of the greatest successes was when I used a cup of chopped dry roasted peanuts left over from a curry supper. Raisins, currants, chopped apple, any kind of nuts or grapenuts cereal, bits of candied or dried fruit (finely chopped) chocolate drops, etc. This recipe is for freezer cookies; the dough is shaped into long rolls, wrapped in a damp tea towel (no foil, please, it's expensive) and stored in the refrigerator or freezer. When you want a few cookies, slice off as many as desired and bake as directed.

FRENCH MADELEINES

You will need madeleine molds for these very special cookies, but it is a good investment in good eating and not expensive. Once purchased it will last for years. They're available in gourmet cookware shops in most cities. If you have trouble finding one write Bazaar de Cuisine, East 56th Street, New York, N.Y. 10022 or the Williams Sonoma Co., Sutter Street, San Francisco, California. While you are at it ask them to send you their catalogues; both are guaranteed to turn even the most diffident cook into and avid amateur chef.

4 eggs, lightly beaten
½ cup granulated sugar
1 cup regular flour (sifted
    before measuring)

1 stick (½ cup) butter, melted
    and cooled to lukewarm
Rind of one small lemon,
    grated

Preheat oven to 400°F.
Butter madeleine molds generously with butter, sprinkle evenly with flour, then shake out any excess.
Combine lightly beaten eggs and sugar in the top half of a double boiler over (not in) barely simmering water. Work together with a wooden spoon until mixture is creamy smooth and sugar has completely dissolved. It should be lukewarm. Remove from heat and beat until cold. Gradually beat in flour,

alternating with lukewarm melted butter. Stir in lemon rind. Pour batter into prepared madeleine molds (about ¾ full) and bake in preheated oven for 25 to 30 minutes or until firm and golden.

Makes about 2 dozen Madeleines

"ANYTHING GOES" COOKIES

1 cup butter (sticks), room
    temperature
½ cup white sugar
½ cup brown sugar
1 egg, well beaten
2½ cups flour

1 tsp. baking soda
1 cup chopped nuts, currants,
    raisins, chopped apple,
    chopped candied or dried
    fruit, etc.

Work the butter in a large mixing bowl with a wooden spoon until it is very light and fluffy. (This can be done with an electric mixer, and it's even easier. Be sure to scrape butter clinging to the beaters back into the bowl.) Add white and brown sugar and beat until light and fluffy and sugar has dissolved. Add beaten egg and stir to blend. Sift flour and soda together. Mix about ½ cup with fruit or nuts to be used. Stir flour mixture into cookie dough, stirring only to blend well. Add floured fruit and nuts. Place mixture in refrigerator to chill until firm enough to handle.

Turn out onto lightly floured board and form into two rolls. Wrap each roll in a damp tea towel and place in freezer. When needed slice off as many cookies as desired and bake on greased cookie sheet in 400°F. oven for 10 to 15 minutes.

Makes about 4 dozen cookies.

APPLESAUCE CAKE

This is an all-time favorite of mine. Moist, fragrant and delicious, it is great plain with tea or coffee or it can be transformed into a gala dessert by the addition of rum-flavored ice cream, hard sauce or whipped cream. It keeps for several weeks in the refrigerator (but I've never known one to last that long at my house). It is also easy to make and virtually foolproof, in addition to being very economical with only 1 stick of butter and 2 eggs for 2 large moist cakes.

2 cups all-purpose flour, sifted
1 cup whole wheat flour, sifted (or use 3 cups regular flour)
2 tsp. baking soda
1 cup nuts, chopped (walnuts, pecan or unsalted roasted peanuts)
1 cup raisins or currants, chopped (or ½ cup of each)
½ cup butter (1 stick), room temperature

¾ cup brown sugar, firmly packed
2 eggs, well beaten
2 cups apple sauce (If fresh applesauce is used it must be made from peeled and cored apples, only lightly sweetened and cooked to a mushy consistency.)
3 tbs. rum or brandy (optional)

Preheat oven to 300°F.

Oil and flour 2 loaf pans.

Sift both flours and baking soda together and set aside. Combine ½ cup flour mixture with nuts and raisins (or currants), mix well to coat fruit and nuts and set aside.

Cream butter until very light and fluffy; add brown sugar and beat until very light and sugar has dissolved. Add the beaten eggs and blend well. Add the flour mixture alternately with the applesauce and if desired, rum or brandy, blending well after each addition. Add fruit and nut mixture and blend well.

Pour into prepared pans and bake in preheated oven for 45 to 50 minutes or until cakes are done.

Turn out onto a wire cake rack and cool thoroughly. Sprinkle with rum or brandy, if desired. Wrap in a damp clean tea towel and store in the refrigerator up to 3 weeks.

SUNSHINE SPONGE CAKE

For the thrifty cook there's no better dessert to have on hand than a nice, big sponge cake. A perfect base for English trifle, lovely with any kind of sauce, great with fresh fruit or ice cream and very good just as is with coffee or tea. Since sponge cake requires no butter and less eggs than angel food, a 10-inch cake (about 12 generous slices) costs less than 75¢.

6 eggs, separated
1 cup cake flour, sifted
⅛ tsp. cream of tartar
1½ cups sugar

½ cup water
1 tbs. orange peel, grated
1 tbs. orange juice

Preheat oven to 325°F.

Separate eggs while cold into two large bowls, making sure not a speck of yolk escapes into the whites. Allow to stand in a fairly warm place (not near heat—the average kitchen temperature is fine) until room temperature and not even a vestige of chill remains. This will take at least an hour. Sift the flour and cream of tartar together and set aside.

Combine the sugar and water in a saucepan and boil over medium heat until it "threads" when dropped from a spoon (soft ball stage on a candy thermometer). Remove from heat and allow to cool slightly. Stir in orange peel and juice.

Beat the egg yolks with a rotary beater or electric mixer until very thick and lemon colored. Using a wire whisk beat the egg whites until very stiff and glossy. Pour the orange-sugar syrup in a fine stream into the beaten egg whites, beating constantly. Fold egg whites into yolks, alternating with flour-cream of tartar mixture. Fold to blend, taking care not to break down egg whites. Pour into ungreased 10-inch tube pan and bake in preheated oven for 50 minutes. Invert on a wire rack to cool for about 15 minutes and then remove from pan.

OEUFS À LA NEIGE

Years ago I used to dine in Lucullan splendor (on my expense account, I hasten to add) at New York's fabled Le Pavillion restaurant. Sadly, the Pavillion is closed and its autocratic owner Henri Soule is dead, but its memory lingers, evergreen, with anyone whoever feasted both wisely and well at what was truly one of the world's great restaurants. What has all this to do with a budget cookbook? A great deal, for like all French restaurants some of their greatest specialities were made from simple and inexpensive ingredients and this was one of my favorite desserts. I think they charged $6 per serving even in those days, but you can make it for small change.

*4 eggs, separated while still
    cold but allowed to come
    to room temperature
1½ cups sugar*

*2 cups milk, scalded
Fresh peaches or strawberries,
    sliced (optional)
Brandy (optional)*

Step one

Beat the egg yolks in the top half of a double boiler until light. Stir in ¼ cup of the sugar, and the hot milk and blend well. Cook over simmering water, stirring constantly, until the custard thickens enough to coat the spoon. Do not overcook. Remove from heat and stir until custard is lukewarm. Cover and store in the refrigerator until ready to assemble dessert.

Step two

Beat the egg whites (with a separate wire whisk) until very stiff but not dry. Gradually beat in ¾ cup of the sugar. Heat a large pot of water to boiling. Using a wet tablespoon form the meringue into egg shapes and slip them off the spoon into the boiling water. Poach for about 2 minutes, then turn and poach the other side 2 minutes. It's best to do just a few at a time. As the "snow eggs" are cooked, lift from the water with a slotted spoon onto absorbent paper to drain.

Step three

Line a large serving bowl (glass is prettiest) with peeled sliced peaches or hulled and sliced strawberries, if desired. Sprinkle fruit with a little brandy. Pour cooled custard over fruit and pile "snow eggs" on top of custard. Refrigerate until ready to serve.

Step four

When ready to serve melt ¼ cup of sugar in a small skillet over very low heat until it is liquid and a light caramel color. With a spoon dribble the caramel over the "snow eggs" where it will harden and add a crisp sweet note to the smoothness of the "snow eggs" and custard. Serve chilled.

Serves 6

Notes

This is not only a fabulously good dessert, but it is amazingly easy. The fruit is purely optional, but if it's summer and the fresh fruit is available, why not? Try it for your next buffet party.

BROILED PEACHES

Use 1 peach for each serving if using fresh peaches. Dip first in boiling water; then with the tip of a sharp knife slip off skins. Cut in half and remove seed. Place in oven-proof dish; sprinkle with sugar and dot with butter. Add about ½ inch of water to the bottom of the pan. Place under broiler and cook until sugar has melted and peaches are soft.

If using canned peaches, allow 2 halves for each serving. Sprinkle halves with sugar, dot with butter and broil until thoroughly heated.

DESSERT RICE RING
FOR SUMMER FRUITS
WITH PEACH PURÉE

This is a party spectacular for pennies. If you want to make it during cold weather months, lightly sugared stewed apple slices can substitute for the fruit and the peach purée.

½ cup rice (brown or regular
    long grain variety)
2 cups milk
3 egg yolks
½ cup sugar
1 tbs. brandy

2 envelopes plain gelatin
2 cups any fresh summer fruit,
    peeled, sliced and lightly
    sugared
Peach Purée (recipe follows)

Place the rice in a heavy saucepan and cover with cold water, bring to a full boil, stir well to separate grains, boil for 2 minutes. Drain the rice in a colander and rinse well with cold water. Return the rice to the saucepan with 1¼ cups of the milk. Cook over low heat until rice is very tender and most of the milk has been absorbed.

Combine the egg yolks and sugar in the top half of a double boiler. Heat the remaining milk to scalding and add to egg-sugar mixture, stirring constantly as it is added. Cook the custard over—not in—simmering water, stirring constantly, until it is thick and smooth. Stir in brandy. Soften the gelatin in a little cold water and add to hot custard. Remove from heat and stir until gelatin is dissolved. Combine cooked rice with custard and blend. Pour into lightly oiled ring mold and chill until firm.

Unmold onto a serving platter and fill center with chilled, sliced and lightly sugared fruit: peaches, strawberries, blueberries, or a combination of two or three. Cover with peach purée and serve.

Notes

If stewed apple slices are to substitute for the summer fruit, chill well before filling ring.

PEACH PURÉE

6 very ripe peaches   1 tbs. brandy
½ tsp. lemon juice   ½ cup sugar

Peel and slice peaches, add remaining ingredients and blend to a purée in a blender or a food mill. Chill until ready to serve.
Serves 6 to 8.

STEWED APPLE SLICES

6 crisp, tart apples   1 cup sugar
Juice from 1 lemon   ¼ cup water
Rind of 1 lemon, grated
    (optional)

Peel, quarter and core the apples, cut into fairly thick slices, place in saucepan with lemon juice, rind, sugar and water. Cook over medium heat until apples are tender. Refrigerate until ready to use.
Makes about 3 cups

BUDGET PEANUT BRITTLE
SOUFFLÉ

1 envelope plain gelatin   4 eggs
2 cups milk   1 cup peanut brittle pieces
½ cup sugar   broken into small bits

This is as elegant a dessert as any cold soufflé, but it's made without the addition of expensive whipping cream, so it's low in calories too.
Soften gelatin in a small amount of cold water. Bring milk

with half the sugar (¼ cup) almost to a boil over medium heat. Pour hot milk over gelatin and stir until gelatin has dissolved. Refrigerate until firm.

Combine the eggs and remaining sugar in the top half of a double boiler over barely simmering water. Beat with a rotary or electric beater until very thick and pale in color. Remove from heat and chill until quite cold.

Place jellied milk mixture in a large mixing bowl and beat with a rotary beater until fluffy; add chilled egg custard and beat until thick and well blended. Add peanut brittle pieces and pour into 1½-quart soufflé mold. Chill until firm.

Serves 6

RUM-NUT ICE CREAM PIE

4 tbs. peanut butter
4 tbs. light brown sugar
2 tbs. light rum
1 pt. vanilla ice cream,
    slightly softened at room
temperature but not
    melted
Graham cracker crumb crust
    (see page 202)
Crushed graham crackers

In a saucepan over low heat melt peanut butter and brown sugar. Remove from heat and stir in rum. Cool slightly, then pour over ice cream and blend as quickly as possible. Spoon into prepared graham cracker crumb crust and sprinkle with crushed graham crackers. Place pie in freezer and freeze until firm.

Serves 6 to 8

PEANUT BUTTER PIE

3 eggs, separated
½ cup peanut butter
1 cup confectioners' sugar
1 9-inch pie shell, baked
¼ cup cornstarch
⅔ cup granulated sugar
¼ cup milk, heated to
    steaming
2 tbs. butter

Separate eggs.

Combine peanut butter with ¾ cup of the confectioners' sugar. Blend with fingers until mixture resembles coarse cornmeal. Spread half the mixture over bottom of baked pie shell.

In a mixing bowl beat egg yolks with cornstarch until blended. Beat in granulated sugar. Gradually add milk, beating as added. Pour into top of double boiler. Cook, stirring, over simmering water until mixture thickens. Add butter and stir until melted. Pour into prepared pie shell.

Beat egg whites until stiff. Fold in remaining confectioners' sugar. Spread over pie filling, covering it completely. Sprinkle with remaining peanut butter mixture.

Bake in preheated 325°F. oven until topping is lightly browned.

Serves 6

RICOTTA CHEESE PIE

8 or 10 graham crackers
1 2-lb. container whole milk
*   ricotta cheese*
1 cup sugar
½ cup candied lemon and
*   orange rind*

¼ cup orange liqueur (or 2
*   tbs. orange juice and 2*
*   tbs. lemon juice)*

Line a 1½-quart, deep baking dish with graham crackers (don't worry about empty spaces). Combine remaining ingredients, pour into baking dish and refrigerate 12 hours or overnight before serving.

Serves 6 to 8

FRIDAY NIGHT PIE

15 saltine crackers
14 dates, cut very fine
1 cup sugar
½ cup corn flakes

1 tsp. orange or lemon rind,
*   grated*
3 egg whites
Vanilla ice cream (optional)

Preheat oven to 300°F.

Crumble crackers, place in electric blender and blend to very fine crumbs (or place in bowl and crush very fine).

Combine crumbs, dates, sugar, corn flakes and grated rind.

Beat egg whites until very stiff and fold into crumb mixture. Pour into a well-buttered 8-inch pie pan. Bake in preheated oven for 45 minutes.

Let stand until cool. Refrigerate until ready to serve.

Serve with vanilla ice cream, if desired.

Serves 6

BLUEBERRY CRUMBLE PIE

4 cups blueberries
1 tbs. lemon juice
2 cups sugar
1/4 lb. butter

1 cup flour
1 1/2 tsp. baking powder
1 cup milk

Preheat oven to 375°F.

Combine blueberries, lemon juice and 1 cup of the sugar; toss to blend.

Melt the butter in a 10-inch square baking pan.

Combine remaining sugar with flour and baking powder. Stir in milk gradually and beat with whisk until smooth. Pour batter into melted butter and mix lightly. Sprinkle evenly with blueberries. Bake in preheated oven for 40 to 45 minutes or until firm and lightly browned. (Blueberries will sink into the batter while baking.)

Serves 6 to 8

PEACH DEEP-DISH PIE
WITH EASY CRACKER CRUST

This is a lovely way to make a delectable deep-dish pie. Easy, quick and inexpensive, it is a perfect ending to a porch supper on a warm summer night.

3 tbs. butter
12 to 14 saltine crackers
1 cup milk (approximately)
3 cups peaches, peeled and
    sliced

½ cup sugar
1 tbs. instant tapioca

Preheat oven to 250°F.

Melt the butter in the preheated oven in a long, flat, shallow baking dish or jelly roll pan. Remove from heat and tilt pan to distribute butter evenly. Crumble crackers into large pieces in the butter in a single layer. Pour milk over crackers. There should be enough milk to soften the crackers, but add more if necessary. Place in preheated oven and bake for 1 hour until crackers are crisp and lightly browned. Remove from pan at once and set aside.

Increase oven temperature to 350°F.

Combine fruit, sugar and tapioca and blend well. Pour fruit mixture into a deep casserole (a 1½-quart soufflé mold is perfect). Bake uncovered for 25 to 30 minutes or until fruit is tender. Cover with prepared cracker pieces and bake for an additional 10 to 15 minutes.

Serve warm with cream cheese whipped until light with a little milk.

Serves 6

ANNABELLE'S SWEET POTATO PONE

Annabelle Stone was a tall black lady of 65 who had lived on John's Island near Charleston, South Carolina, all of her life. She had a farm and ran a night club; she also consented to "help me out" two days a week. In addition to showing me how to make peach peeling wine and horse melon chutney, she demonstrated this sweet potato pone much to the enjoyment of myself and any fortunate friends who came for dinner. It is a lovely and cheap dessert.

¼ cup butter, very soft   1 tbs. brandy
1 cup brown sugar   2 tbs. orange juice
3 eggs, lightly beaten   2 tbs. orange rind, grated
2 cups sweet potatoes, grated

Preheat oven to 300°F.

Cream the butter and sugar together until light and fluffy; add eggs and blend. Add sweet potatoes and all remaining ingredients. Beat well to blend. Pour into a buttered baking dish and bake in preheated oven for 1 hour. Serve warm with cream, ice cream, or just as is.

Serves 6

COMPOTE OF WINTER FRUIT

3 large McIntosh apples   ½ cup sugar
1 cup pitted cooked prunes   ½ cup dry white wine (or
½ cup raisins   substitute by increasing
3 large navel oranges   orange juice to 1 cup)
½ cup orange juice

Peel and core the apples and cut into fairly thick slices; place in a large nonmetal bowl. Add pitted prunes and raisins. Cut oranges into even, fairly thick slices; with kitchen shears remove rind and white pith. Cut each slice into quarters. Add to fruit in bowl. Add sugar, orange juice and wine. Allow to marinate for at least 6 hours. Serve at room temperature.

Serves 4 to 6

SNOW PUDDING

2 envelopes unflavored gelatin   ½ cup sugar
¼ cup cold water   1 qt. vanilla ice cream
2 cups canned crushed   Pineapple rings (optional)
    pineapple

Soften gelatin in cold water. Heat pineapple and sugar, stirring frequently until sugar has dissolved and mixture is almost boiling. Stir in softened gelatin until dissolved. Chill until quite thick. Stir in softened ice cream and blend well. Pour into decorative mold that has first been rinsed with cold water. Chill until firm. Unmold and keep chilled until ready to serve.

Note

To make unmolding easier, wrap bottom of mold with a hot wet towel. Unmold on plate rinsed with cold water and mold will slide easily into place. Garnish with pineapple rings if desired.

Serves 8

A few old-fashioned dessert favorites from the days when a good housewife's motto was "Use it up—make it do—or do without," and children were satisfied with a two-penny allowance. Bonus: these desserts taste as delicious as ever.

INDIAN PUDDING

5 cups reconstituted dry skim
   milk (Regular milk may
   be used and if so, skip the
   butter; but this version is
   cheaper.)
2 tbs. butter
1 cup yellow cornmeal (Try
   for the old-fashioned
   stone-ground variety
   without preservatives,

   usually available in
   health food stores.)
1 cup molasses
1 tsp. salt
1 tsp. lemon rind, grated
¼ tsp. baking soda
2 eggs, lightly beaten
2 tbs. brandy (my own
   addition)

Preheat oven to 250°F.

Place milk in top half of a double boiler and bring to just below boiling over medium heat. Remove from heat, stir in butter and cornmeal. Place over (not in) gently simmering water and cook, stirring occasionally, for about 20 minutes. Remove from heat and stir in all remaining ingredients. Pour into lightly greased baking dish and bake in slow preheated oven for 3 hours. Serve warm with cold milk or sprinkled with a bit of brandy.

Serves 6 to 8

TAPIOCA CUSTARDS

Do you remember tapioca custard? We had it often as children during the depression—or maybe you're too young to remember it. Tapioca custards are a delicate, delicious ending to any meal; just don't explain how cheap it is and everyone will love it.

Here's the classic recipe and a few variations:

½ *cup quick-cooking tapioca* ¼ *tsp. salt*
2 *cups milk* ⅓ *cup sugar*
2 *eggs, separated and allowed* 1 *tsp. vanilla (or brandy)*
  to come to room
  temperature

Combine the tapioca and milk in the top half of a double boiler and cook over simmering water, stirring often, until tapioca is clear. Remove from heat. Beat the yolks until thick; add salt and sugar and beat to blend well. Add to milk and tapioca mixture and return to heat. Cook over simmering water until it begins to thicken. Remove from heat and allow to cool. Stir in flavoring. Beat egg whites until stiff and fold into custard. Serve cold, plain or with variations below.

Serves 4 to 6

Variations

Serve over sliced ripe peaches, strawberries, bananas, fresh pineapple, blueberries, etc. For extra flavor sprinkle fruit lightly with sugar and brandy and allow to stand for at least an hour at room temperature before serving with ice cold custard. (Sprinkle bananas first with lemon juice to prevent turning brown.)

Fold shaved bits of bitter chocolate into each serving.

Melt a few pieces of peanut brittle with a little water to a liquid and pour over chilled custard.

Serve with orange peel sauce (see page 200).

Stir a tablespoon of grapenuts into each portion and serve with brandy-flavored whipped cream.

OLD-FASHIONED RICE PUDDING

This is the creamy delicate kind, good enough to be served solo but even more delectable with Orange Peel Sauce (see below). Only one word of caution here: you cannot spend extra money to buy so-called converted rice to make this because it won't break down to a smooth creaminess. For the kind of results you want, you'll have to spend less on plain old regular long grain or buy natural brown rice.

½ cup rice	¼ tsp. salt
½ cup sugar	4 cups milk

Preheat oven to 250°F.

Mix ingredients in a large bowl, pour into buttered baking dish (one with a cover) cover and bake 2 to 2½ hours. Uncover the last 10 minutes of baking to brown lightly. Serve warm with Orange Peel Sauce (recipe follows).

Serves 4 to 6

ORANGE PEEL SAUCE

This is simply delicious over rice custard, ice cream or baked custard and it costs only pennies. Remember how many orange rinds you have thrown away? I make a quart at a time. Pour it in jars and keep in my refrigerator for up to 2 weeks. It's lovely to have on hand.

Rinds from 6 or 7 large oranges	*2 cups sugar*
Water	*2 cups water*
	1 tbs. brandy (optional)

Cut the orange rinds into julienne strips, as evenly as possible. Place in a saucepan and add cold water to cover. Bring to a boil over high heat, pour off and discard water. Repeat the process, for this removes any bitterness from the peel.

Combine sugar and water in a saucepan, bring to a boil and stir until sugar has dissolved. Add orange peel and cook over medium heat, stirring occasionally, until syrup thickens slightly and orange strips are tender, about 30 minutes. Stir in brandy. Cool, pour into jars, cover and refrigerate until ready to serve.

Makes about 2 cups

APPLE BETTY

When winter doldrums set in after Christmas and apples are plentiful and cheap, I make apple betty. Served warm with a wedge of cheese, it is a wonderful dessert.

6 medium-size tart apples	*wheat which has more*
1 cup brown sugar	*flavor)*
1 cup flour (I like to use whole	*3 tbs. butter*

Preheat oven to 250°F.

Peel, quarter and core the apples, cut into medium-thick

slices. Place slices, overlapping, in a shallow baking dish. Combine sugar, flour and butter in a mixing bowl and mix together until crumbly. Sprinkle evenly over apples in baking dish. Bake in slow preheated oven for 1 hour or until apples are tender.

Serve warm with a little brandy or with milk.

Serves 6

APPLE PIE WITH WHEAT GERM AND BROWN SUGAR TOPPING

Pastry for one 9-inch pie pan
(recipe follows)
6 to 8 McIntosh apples
1 tbs. lemon juice
¾ cup sugar
½ tsp. cinnamon
¼ tsp. allspice

1 tsp. lemon rind, grated
(optional)
¼ cup margarine or butter
(room temperature)
½ cup brown sugar, packed
down
½ cup wheat germ

Peel, core and cut the apples into fairly thin slices, place in a large mixing bowl and sprinkle with lemon juice to prevent discoloring. Add sugar, spices and lemon rind. Mix well and allow to stand for 1 or 2 hours to draw out the natural sugar and juice from the apples.

Preheat oven to 400°F.

Line a 9-inch pie plate with pastry and fill with apples rounding, evenly on top.

Mix softened butter or margarine with brown sugar and wheat germ until "crumbly." Sprinkle evenly over apples.

Place pie in preheated oven and immediately lower heat to 300°F. Bake for about 45 minutes or until fruit is soft and top is lightly browned. Serve warm or at room temperature.

Serves 6 to 8

NEVER-FAIL QUICK
PASTRY FOR ONE 9-INCH PIE PAN

½ cup shortening
¼ cup water
1½ cups flour

½ tsp. baking powder
½ tsp. salt

Melt shortening; add water and mix with remaining ingredients to form a soft dough. Using floured hands, roll into a ball and chill for at least two hours. Roll out on a floured pastry board to about ¼- to ⅛-inch thickness and line pie pan with pastry, fluting edges with fingertips. Chill until ready to use.

Note

For best results roll out on a floured pastry canvas using a rolling pin covered with a floured mit. These are generally available in housewares departments.

GRAHAM CRACKER CRUST

2 cups Graham Cracker
    crumbs

½ cup (1 stick) butter or
    margarine (room
    temperature)
½ cup sugar

Preheat oven to 300°F.

Combine crumbs, softened butter and sugar and mix well. Press evenly onto bottom and sides of a 9-inch pie pan. Bake in preheated oven for 10 minutes. Cool before using.

SUMMER
BLUEBERRY PUDDING

8 to 10 slices firm white bread
2 tbs. butter
4 cups blueberries

1½ cups sugar
¼ tsp. salt

Remove the crusts from the bread and butter one side of each slice. Butter a round-bottom bowl and line it with half of the bread, buttered side up.

Combine blueberries and sugar in a saucepan and cook over medium heat until sugar is dissolved. Pour over bread slices in bowl. Cover with remaining bread slices, buttered side down. Weight the pudding with a heavy plate. If necessary, fill a plastic bag with uncooked rice and place on the plate to weigh it down. Refrigerate for at least 24 hours. The bread will absorb the juice and the pudding may be easily unmolded. It is a beautiful sight on a summer day.

Serve with a spoonful of whipped or sour cream.

Serves 6

LEMON-CHEESE MOUSSE

1 cup cottage cheese
1 cup sour cream
½ cup confectioners' sugar
1 tsp. lemon rind, grated

Orange peel sauce (see page 200) or any homemade jam or preserves (strawberry preserves are especially good)

Put cottage cheese, sour cream, confectioners' sugar in electric blender and blend until smooth. Stir in grated lemon rind. Spoon into sherbert glasses and chill several hours.

Top with orange peel sauce or preserves just before serving.

Serves 4 to 6

COTTAGE CHEESE
FRUIT DUMPLINGS

Here is a really unusual dessert that's easy and inexpensive. A lovely ending to a vegetable dinner I might add.

2 tbs. soft butter
2 tbs. sugar
2 eggs, lightly beaten
2 cups (1 pt.) cottage cheese,
    well drained
3 cups flour

¼ cup milk (approximately)
3 cups uncooked peaches or
    apples, peeled and
    chopped
Sour cream

Cream the butter and sugar together until light and fluffy; add the eggs and mix well. Add cottage cheese and beat well to blend. Add the flour alternately with the milk to make a soft dough. Roll out on a floured board and cut into 1½-inch squares. Place a spoonful of the prepared fruit in the center of half of the squares, cover with a second square, sealing the edges firmly with a fork first dipped in hot water. Bring a large kettle of water to a full boil and drop the dumplings into it a few at a time. Boil for about 8 minutes or until dumplings rise to the top. Remove and drain in a colander.

Serve warm with sour cream or Peach Purée (see page 191) and plenty of hot coffee.

Makes about 16 dumplings

ENTREMENT PAIN PERDUE
(Dessert French Toast)

1 cup dried prunes
2 tbs. sugar
½ tsp. lemon rind, grated
1 tbs. brandy
12 slices firm white bread

4 eggs, beaten with 3 tbs.
    water
4 tbs. butter
Confectioners' sugar

Put prunes in a saucepan and cover with water. Let soak several hours or overnight. Place over low heat and let simmer until very soft. Drain, remove pits and mash to a purée. Stir in sugar, lemon rind and brandy.

Trim crust from the bread. Spread half the slices with the prune mixture and cover with remaining slices. Dip each sandwich in beaten egg.

Fry each sandwich in about 2 tsp. sizzling butter in a heavy skillet, turning once, until lightly browned. Sprinkle each with confectioners' sugar. Keep warm in 300°F. oven until all are prepared.

Serves 6

SHORTCAKE

Who could dream of a more delectable dessert than shortcake? And if you use in-season fruit (there we go again), it's just about as cheap as gelatin. Need I explain why most people prefer it?

Here is an absolutely never-fail batch of biscuit "receipt" from Savannah, Georgia. Make it up; use some for tonight and store the rest for use during the next week or 10 days. Shortcake biscuits don't have to be hot, you know; in fact, room temperature is best with lots of cut up fresh fruit that has been sliced into a bowl, lightly sugared and left to stand at room temperature for an hour or so to bring out the juices. Strawberries and peaches are my favorite shortcake fruits, but there's no harm in a winter apple shortcake made by cooking peeled, crisp apples slices in a sugar syrup (to which you have added a grating of lemon rind and a spoonful or so of brandy) until they are just tender. Serve warm, please.

SAVANNAH BISCUITS

2 cups all-purpose flour   3 tbs. vegetable shortening
4 tsp. baking powder   ¾ cup milk
1 tsp. salt

Preheat oven to 450°F.

Sift dry ingredients into a large bowl, cut shortening into flour mixture (use a pastry blender if available; if not a fork will do) until the mixture resembles fine cornmeal. Make a well in the center and pour milk in all at once. Stir lightly with a fork until just blended. Using a *light* touch, form dough into a ball and place on *lightly* floured board. Roll out gently—don't press down. Cut out biscuits with a round biscuit cutter dipped first in flour. Place on lightly greased cookie sheet (just touching to make them rise) and bake in preheated oven 10 to 15 minutes or until golden brown.

Makes about 1 dozen large biscuits.

CREAM PUFFS

Cream puffs can be baked, frozen and then filled just before serving; or they can be filled with any appropriate ice cream or flavored, sweetened whipped cream, and then frozen and served with any compatible sauce. They can be made one-bite size or large enough for one serving; or they can be fried (without filling), dusted with confectioners' sugar and served hot or cold. What's more, part can be baked and then set aside to be frozen and filled with creamed chicken, crab meat or any mixture suitable for a main course or hors d'oeuvers.

PÂTÉ À CHOU
(Basic Cream Puff Pastry)

1 cup water   *1 cup flour*
½ cup butter   *5 eggs*
½ teaspoon salt

Place butter and water in a saucepan, bring to a full boil, and add salt and flour all at once. Stir vigorously until dough is smooth and does not cling to the sides of the pan. Remove from heat and add eggs one at a time, beating until smooth and glossy.

Drop rounds of dough from teaspoon or tablespoon, depending on the size of puff desired (or force through a pastry tube), onto a greased cookie sheet. Bake for 10 minutes at 400°F., then reduce heat to 325°F. for 15 to 20 minutes. Puffs should be light to the hand and light golden brown in color. If you are not sure they are are right, simply take one and test it. If necessary, bake them a few minutes longer, covered lightly with foil to prevent further browning.

Notes

This is both an easy and a difficult pastry. The dough will be stiff at first and hard to manage, but the secret of light and airy puffs is in the beating, so don't skimp. That 1 or 2 minutes of work means the difference between failure and success.

PROFITEROLES AU CHOCOLAT

Cool puffs thoroughly and cut a slit in the side of each. Fill with vanilla ice cream flavored lightly, if desired, with rum. Freeze on a flat tray until firm, pack in a container or plastic bag and store in the freezer until ready to serve.

To serve

Thaw at room temperature for 10 minutes. Serve with heated chocolate sauce made by combining 2 squares melted, unsweetened chocolate with ½ cup sugar; blend well. Add ½ cup milk and cook over low heat, stirring constantly, until thick and smooth.

CRÊPES

Now what's Spartan about Crêpes Suzette for dessert? They sound sinfully rich, but the truth is they cost almost nothing per serving. They are not only easy to make, but you can make up batch and freeze them (allow to cool on a rack, place in stacks of 12, a piece of waxed paper between each crêpe, wrap securely and freeze). Simple? Of course.

I've given a recipe for crêpes Suzette here, but they can also be a really great luncheon or supper dish filled with creamed chicken or tuna fish, sprinkled with grated cheese and baked until hot and the cheese has melted.

BASIC CRÊPES

2 eggs	½ tsp. vanilla
Pinch of salt	¾ cup flour
1 tsp. sugar	2 tbs. butter, melted and
1 cup milk	cooled

Beat eggs until light and "lemony." Blend in salt, sugar, milk, and vanilla. Add flour and beat with a wire whisk until batter is smooth. Blend in melted butter. Let batter stand 1 or 2 hours before making crêpes.

Grease a 5- or 6-inch crêpe pan generously with soft butter. Heat to sizzling. Pour in a generous tablespoon of batter; quickly rotate and tilt pan so that batter completely covers bottom in a thin layer. Cook over medium heat until brown on bottom, turn to brown other side. Turn out and repeat until all batter has been used. Keep crêpes warm in a very low oven, covered with an inverted bowl, until ready to serve. Serve dusted with confectioners' sugar, or with honey, jam or syrup, or make Crêpes Suzette.

Makes 18 to 20 crêpes

CRÊPES SUZETTE

Now that you've mastered crêpes, here's the classic Suzette sauce. If you have a chafing dish, it's fun to make them at the table.

12 crêpes (see Basic Crêpes
   page 208)
4 tbs. sugar (or 4 lumps of loaf
   sugar)

Juice from 2 oranges
5 tbs. butter, room
   temperature
½ cup + 2 tbs. brandy

Place the crêpes in an oven-proof dish to warm in 200°F. oven until ready to use.

Combine the sugar and 2 tbs. of the orange juice; then blend in 2 tbs. of the butter. Heat remaining orange juice in a flat skillet or chafing dish pan; add the ½ cup of brandy. When mixture boils, add butter-sugar mixture and stir to blend. Place crêpes in the sauce, spooning it over them liberally. Fold each crêpe into triangles, pour remaining brandy over crepes, ignite and serve as soon as flame dies out.

Serves 4

Bits and Pieces

Waste not, want not, is an old fashioned saying, but it still holds true, especially when it comes to saving money on grocery bills. It's been said that Americans could feed half the starving people of the world out of their garbage cans. Probably true and in these days of high-priced food it's important not to waste a scrap. The problem is what do you do with those bits and pieces? I've spent some time asking the good cooks I know and doing a bit of experimenting on my own and here are the results for you to try. I hope to spur you on to more ideas of your own.

• Spread bite-size cubes of leftover pot roast, braised pork, baked ham or what have you with homemade mustard (see page 178). Top each cube with a small slice of crisp pickle and spear with a cocktail pick. Serve as hors d'oeuvre.

• Spear bite-size cubes of leftover cooked pork with cocktail picks. Serve as appetizers with leftover tomato sauce and horseradish mixed half and half as a dip.

• Cook a mixture of fresh vegetables in beef or chicken stock and add diced leftover meat, chicken or turkey. Season with a bit of dry mustard. If desired, thicken stock with a little flour kneaded with a bit of butter for a delicious, quick-to-make stew.

● Add diced leftover meat to potato salad or combine with chopped ripe tomatoes; bind with mayonnaise and serve on crisp lettuce leaves.

● Add diced leftover meat, chicken, or turkey to tomato sauce or other sauces. Serve over pasta, rice or potatoes.

● Cut leftover beef or pork into finger strips. Add enough sour cream to coat meat. Serve as hors d'oeuvres with cocktail picks for spearing.

● Chop leftover pot roast with crisp cucumber pickles. Moisten with gravy or stock, season with Worcestershire sauce. Use as sandwich spread.

● Mash hot, freshly boiled potatoes with leftover, reheated pot roast gravy instead of butter or cream. Fold in chopped leftover pot roast. Shape into cakes. Place under broiler heat until browned. Spoon gravy over and serve as main course.

● Add 2 or 3 tbs. pot roast gravy or beef stock to water when cooking rice. Drain rice, mix with diced, leftover pot roast. Do the same with leftover chicken or turkey gravy or stock, and chicken or turkey meat.

● Mix finely diced baked or braised ham with equal parts chopped hard-cooked egg. Bind with mayonnaise thinned with a bit of vinegar; add salt and pepper to taste. Serve on lettuce leaves.

● Mix leftover baked or braised ham or pork with cold, cooked lima beans and chopped mild onion. Spoon into scooped-out tomato shells. Garnish with mayonnaise and serve on lettuce leaves.

● Spread bread first with cranberry jelly, then with minced leftover chicken or turkey. Cover with second slice of bread and spread with horseradish. Toast both sides. Spoon hot gravy over surface.

● Add thin strips of roasted leftover turkey or chicken to clear soup or broth, creamed soup or to chef's or potato salad.

• Mix equal parts leftover roast chicken or turkey and minced celery and green pepper; quickly fork-stir into jellied consommé.

• Add flaked leftover poached or broiled fish to potato and leek soup or any vegetable soup.

• Cover chunks of cold leftover poached or broiled fish with chili sauce. Place on lettuce-lined plates with wedges of hard-cooked egg and fresh tomato, pickled beet or dilly beans. Serve as a seafood antipasto.

• Add flaked poached or broiled fish to a rich cream sauce. Spoon over steamed broccoli on freshly made, hot, buttered toast—an easy but elegant luncheon.

• Add leftover cooked vegetables and leftover cooking liquid to freshly cooked vegetables 1 or 2 minutes before they are ready to take from the stove: green beans to diced carrots, stewed tomatoes to spinach, lima beans to kernel corn, kernel corn to cauliflower and so on.

• Purée leftover cooked vegetables and leftover cooking liquid in electric blender; add to cream sauce for chicken, seafood or vegetables.

• Reheat chopped or diced leftover cooked vegetables in a bit of butter; add lightly beaten egg and scramble. Serve on lightly toasted bread spread with deviled ham.

• Reheat leftover cooked vegetables in butter. Combine with freshly cooked flat noodles. Toss with plenty of grated Parmesan cheese.

• Purée leftover cooked vegetables and their liquid in electric blender. Combine with equal parts cottage cheese. Season with salt. Scoop out centers of freshly baked potatoes and mash with vegetable-cheese mixture. Add a little grated Parmesan cheese if you have some. Fill shells with mixture and reheat.

• To each cup of cold leftover kidney beans, lima beans or any boiled beans, add ½ cup chopped celery and green pepper. Toss with vinaigrette dressing. Let stand an hour or so at room temperature. Serve as a salad. Add, if you have them, chopped radishes and crisp, chopped pickle.

• Reheat leftover boiled beans in a spicy tomato sauce, or cream sauce with cheese.

• Peel and chop leftover baked apples and add to fruit salad; or dice and mix into any cold cereal before adding sugar and milk; or peel and mash with a little brandy or apple cider to serve over scoops of vanilla ice cream.

• Mix leftover applesauce with cottage cheese; add chopped roasted peanuts. Pile in the center of lettuce-lined plates. Surround with diced fresh fruit. A little French dressing goes over all.

• Grapes—those last few—add to both fruit and green salad, of course, but also to a salad of chicken or turkey; or slice and remove seeds and add to steamed brussels sprouts or chopped broccoli; or add to a cream sauce for fish.

• To that little bit of jam or jelly in the jar, add a bit of brandy, apple cider or white wine. Cover jar and shake vigorously. Use as is or heat. Serve as sauce over ice cream, custard or cake.

• Add the last handful of raisins to fruit salad or sprinkle over green salad. Stir into hot, cooked cereal, add to custards, cookie and muffin batter or to biscuit dough. Add to curry sauce. Stir with grated orange rind into hot, just-cooked rice.

• Grate any leftover hard cheese. Pack in small containers and freeze. Use frozen. Stir into sauces, sprinkle over soup or au gratin dishes. Toss with pasta or fork-stir into hot rice.

Frozen grated cheese will stay fresh almost indefinitely. You can keep adding grated cheese to same container. Stir to blend each time you add.

• Mash leftover baked beans. Combine with chili sauce or piccadilli and spread on buttered rye bread for a terrific sandwich. Mash beans into hot mashed potatoes, place in a baking dish and sprinkle with grated American or cheddar cheese; place under high broiler heat until cheese melts. Mash beans, bind with beaten egg (1 egg to each 2 cups of beans); form into small flat cakes. Sauté in butter turning once, until crisp. Serve with syrup or honey.

Index